CW01648713

"I am so grateful to The Actors Workshop Online. Tim's teaching has helped me hone my craft and taught me skills that have helped me build a career in the acting industry."

Steph Lacey, actor, *Stay Close* (Netflix)

"Sara knows exactly what a great monologue needs and I should know, she helped me land my first agent! A monologue book curated by Sara and Tim is gold for any actor looking to build a showreel."

Jo Barker, actor, Triforce MonologueSlam finalist.

This book and the monologues contained within are the copyright of The Actors Workshop Online. The monologues can be performed anywhere in the world free of charge, providing The Actors Workshop Online and relevant authors are publicly credited.

All rights reserved. This book may not be duplicated or reproduced. This book is not for re-sale. Any commercial use of this book and/or its contents is strictly prohibited without prior consent of The Actors Workshop Online.

For all enquiries please email: contact@theactorsworkshopnottingham.com

Copyright © The Actors Workshop Online.
The moral rights of the authors have been asserted.
Published in the United Kingdom by Alruna.

Curated and edited by Sara Bodinar and Tim Bryn Smith.
Cover design (featuring Claire Waterall) by Tim Bryn Smith.

ISBN number: 978-1-8384335-0-5

CONTENTS

Talking to my Therapist

Monologues About Grief

On the Verge of a New Life

Unlucky in Love

Monologues About Family

Revelations

Crime and Legal

FOREWORD

Do you know how many times a day agents and casting directors have to sit through Belize's monologue from *Angels in America*? A lot! As an auditioning actor, you can easily stand out from the crowd and make yourself more memorable, simply by choosing something more original to perform.

I was thrilled when Tim asked me to edit and co-curate this compilation of original monologues with him. Having been involved with both writing and casting via the film studios and theatres I work for, I can fully appreciate that there's an appetite for original words that simply isn't being fulfilled.

These monologues are for you to use in your auditions and showreels. They were written by members of the workshop following a series of classes that guided the actors in how to give their stories maximum impact. Practising storytelling skills is important for every actor, but through committing their own words to paper, members also gained a greater insight into what it takes to make a monologue script compelling, dramatic and populated with richly layered, distinct and colourful characters. You will find options for different genders and ages in this collection.

Personally, I developed my lifelong passion for writing and stagecraft aged nine running around the warren of dressing rooms in St John's Hall in Penzance, waiting to be called to the stage. I was a member of a drama group which performed regular variety shows. We sang and danced our way through all the hits of the musicals and sometimes, thrillingly, even had a classic line or two to perform. None of it was original, but that wasn't the nature of what we were doing. What it did do was make me long to be the one who put new dramatic words in the mouths of others, and present fresh ideas to the audience.

I'm not alone in wanting to do this and certainly not the only person in a position to do it. We are all creative in our own way and we all have a story to tell. Being motivated to write is all that's required to take that first step towards a more creative future.

Harnessing creativity in others is a skill in its own right and Tim Bryn Smith, founder of The Actors Workshop, is truly a master at this. This is what makes his classes and projects so enjoyable, exciting, eye-opening, and full of performance possibility. In the friendly, supportive space he creates, I've seen members evolve into happier, confident, more creative individuals, not to mention more accomplished actors.

We hope you enjoy these monologues and find them inspiring in your quest for better castings, better showreels and altogether better acting prospects. If they help you land the part, please do get in touch with us. We'd love to share them on social media and help you celebrate your success.

Sara Bodinar

Writer-in-Residence at The Actors Workshop Online

WHAT IS A SHOWREEL?

As an actor, a showreel is your main promotional tool. It's a video portfolio of your best work, usually no longer than three minutes, and contains clips from TV shows, films and commercials you've been involved in.

Obtaining footage can be challenging, so newer actors often film themselves performing monologues and short scenes for inclusion in their showreels. A great showreel should not only platform you and your ability, but also reveal your casting "types", giving some indication of your acting range in an efficient, engaging way. Actors should regularly update their showreels, replacing older sections with better, more recent work.

A showreel is the industry's measure of your suitability for a potential role and, more broadly speaking, your talent and experience as an actor. Casting directors, producers or directors will often draw up a shortlist of suitable actors for a role by first reviewing a selection of showreels. The actors that meet the criteria are invited to audition, either in person or via self-tape. Actors can sometimes even be cast on the strength of their showreels alone. For the best roles on stage and screen, there will always be a high number of actors in consideration. That's why it's so important that your showreel presents you to the best of your ability and helps you to stand out from the crowd. Having an awesome showreel is one of the best ways to get yourself noticed.

Once you've reached a certain level of profile and experience, your "name" might be enough to land you a role. Leonardo DiCaprio and Dame Judi Dench do not have to tout their showreels to get cast anymore. But it takes time and hard work to build a profile. For new actors starting out, it's a showreel that gets their foot in the door.

What to include in a showreel?

Be brutal when it comes to selecting material for your showreel, because it's definitely a case of "less is more". Your showreel should only contain short clips of your finest work, with your most engaging footage placed at the beginning. It's the first ten seconds that count, so you need to start your monologue with a compelling statement or "hook" that will engage a casting director and keep them watching.

New actors often work on independent or student films in order to gather showreel material. However, tracking down the footage from these types of projects can often be tricky, plus there are no guarantees of the audio and visual quality. Avoiding these pitfalls is the reason many new actors embark on sourcing or producing their own showreel material. By creating your own showreel footage, you can tailor it to suit your type and include a wide emotional range, showcasing all of your unique abilities. With YouTube now issuing severe warnings to anyone posting monologues extracted from published plays, it's even more important to source scripts that won't breech copyright terms.

Camera equipment and editing software are readily available these days, and you can pretty much learn all the basic skills from free video tutorials. New smart phones offer 4k video capabilities with integrated editing software, so it's easy to produce showreel footage of a very high quality on a shoestring budget. All you need to produce your own showreel footage is a few great scripts.

Monologues for showreels

In this book, you'll find a broad selection of monologues suited for a wide range of ages and genders. If there's a script you like, but it's the wrong age or gender, you can always change the character details to make it more suited to your casting type. The objective is to get the most out of the material, so have fun, play around and experiment with the text, even if this means changing the lines. The most important thing is that the words fit you like a glove. So, if you would personally phrase a particular line differently, then feel free to change it, to fit your own turn of phrase or dialect.

When it comes to filming a monologue, think about how you can include a few short cutaways of the other character(s) you are talking to. There's nothing to stop you enlisting a fellow actor, friend, or even a family member. You could ask them to ad-lib a few response lines, so that you can upscale the look and production value of your showreel.

Writing your own monologues

At The Actors Workshop Online, we run classes on how to write showreel monologues. In fact, most of the authors featured in this book developed their monologues as a result of our script writing workshops. Whilst we have carefully curated a wide selection of monologues in this book, you could always consider writing your own monologues to ensure the material featured in your showreel is a perfect fit for you and your casting type.

If you decide to embark on writing a monologue of your own, here's a few things to consider:

- What kind of characters suit your casting types? Casting directors want to know what you do best, especially early in your career. So, work with material that suits your type. Most actors begin by playing versions of themselves until they have a proven track record.
- What types of situations, relationships or topics compel you? What themes or ideas can you relate to? If you really connect deeply to the material, it's likely you will bring your own unique quality to the work. Also, what life experiences could you bring to your performances that add emotional truth and depth to your work?
- Do you have a preference for comedy or drama, and which do you play best? A great monologue often has a blend of both.
- What material can you include that feels original and hasn't been seen before in other actors' showreels?

- Monologues that show one emotion won't maintain an audience's interest or showcase your acting talent. Try to include an emotional climax or turning point. A revelatory moment in your monologue, when the character has a realisation or discovers something new, will give you the chance to display a variety of emotions.
- Make your monologue suit your own voice and language. A strong character voice in a monologue can go a long way to adding colour, interest and perspective to the piece. If you feel at home in the character's words, then your performance will be both real and authentic.
- Where possible, look for emotional contrast. I've seen so many monologues where actors try to showcase dramatic acting skills by performing a "sad" scene in a predictably "sad" way. They begin with a melancholy voice and matching facial expression, then inevitably build up to lots of weeping. But emotional complexity is far more compelling; audiences connect more deeply when a character tries to hold back tears. Find ways to play the opposite emotion to the words you are saying. When a character is telling a traumatic story, begin with a smile or some laughter. Not only does this provide an emotional contrast to the lines you are saying but it will give your character the chance to demonstrate that all-important emotional turning point, when suddenly a brave smile fades and the tears start to stream.

Reaching the next level in your career

Regardless of whether you're starting out in your career as an actor, or you're simply looking to refresh your showreel, we're confident that the material contained in this book, used effectively, will provide you with an alluring portfolio to help sell your skills to industry decision-makers and reach your next professional milestone.

To find out more about our services, keep in touch with The Actors Workshop Online. We offer a variety of courses for all experience levels and abilities, as well as one-to-one advanced tuition and screen acting crash courses. Break a leg!

Tim Bryn Smith

Founder & Director, The Actors Workshop Online

Life and Death Monologues

YOU STILL TERRIFY ME by Clare McGill

Sandra is at the hospital, sitting beside her unconscious elderly mother.

SANDRA: I used to be scared of you when I was younger. Terrified at times! Your sharp, thunderous voice used to penetrate the walls and shake the house, when you shouted upstairs to me. I used to imagine flames billowing out of your mouth.

Oh God! What have I done now? More's to the point, what's my punishment going to be? How is your anger going to burn me this time? And is there anything I can do to stop it? I'm not sure what I've done yet, but if only I could wind back the clock and un-do it, no question, I would!

I used to rebel against you when I was a teenager. Not that I'd ever let you see. I'd do things like clean the toilet with your toothbrush, or spit in your tea because I was angry when you used to make me do chores for being "obtuse". Can you ever forgive me?

I understand you a bit better now I'm older. You've told me stories about how you used to get the cane, or the slipper, or the belt for doing next to nothing. I'm sorry you had to put up with that... But so did I!

History repeats itself.

I used to be scared of you when I was younger… but here you are now looking so old, frail, and delicate in that hospital bed. Now the thing that scares me the most is the thought of you not being around. You slipping away terrifies me more than anything you've ever done before.

OUR OPTIONS by Conor McGee

Phil is talking to the doctor who is explaining the course of action they need to take regarding his terminally ill mother.

PHIL: Sorry but now you've said your little piece, can you stop calling these our "options". You can wrap it up in any doctor-talk you want, but options imply there's an actual bloody choice to make here, doesn't it? Choice means that you can affect the outcome, and from what you just said, it won't, will it?

You just offered different ways to get to the same place, the same result...her, dying, in this hospital bed. You didn't say anything about her getting better, or her coming home to her family. An offer of this medication and of that medication, but nothing that will actually help my mum get better.

I don't care about slowing the cancer down, I want it gone. I want her better. And if you can't offer that, then there's no choice on the table that I can take.

Those can't be our only options. Also, can you stop calling them "our" options? Because from where I'm standing, you've come in, made your little announcement about which option you're going to prepare for and now you've asked us to confirm that we're on board with it.

We're not on board with it. In fact, I've come here to offer you an option; the option to be honest. I get it. It's my mother. She's very ill. Tell me directly the most effective way to make her final days as bearable as possible and don't dress it up in this clinical training manual speak. Talk to me like it's your mother. We're all busy but showing empathy to both of us takes less than a minute. Please.

IT IS WHAT IT IS by Ángeles Clares Cruz

Antonia is lying in her bedroom looking at Instagram. She has just had some bad news and so calls her friend to get it off her chest.

ANTONIA: I've just seen your wedding on Instagram. A new husband? Good girl! You didn't waste any time. Sorry, I can't remember his name...? Déjame pensar… Mark, Peter, Freddie? Tom! Oh yes. Tom looked stunning.

Do I sound weird? I'm not hiding anything. I never got married although he did pop the question. Of course I said no. He knew I would. I warned him for 10 years that if he asked, I'd decline. So, you see the reason I didn't go to your wedding is not because I'm sad I'm not married. It's because I had an appointment with my ginecólogo that I couldn't postpone. I cannot have babies. That's what he told me. I'm not married. And I can't have babies. But that's okay. I am still a strong Latino woman. Just because I can't have a baby, or don't want to get married, does not mean I am less of a woman.

He always wanted to have a baby. But I did not. He would call this a "curse". But, for me, it's a relief. I know you're struggling to believe me, but please open your mind and accept we are different. This is the best outcome. I'm not going to hide how I feel anymore.

PERFECT by Gill Cooke

Liz confides in her best friend.

LIZ: I wasn't even sure I wanted to be a mum. That first night after I had the twins, well, I had never felt so happy and so exhausted at the same time. I knew I needed to sleep but I just couldn't stop looking at them. Their perfect little mouths. Their beautiful little button noses. I'd push my face right in to their soft little necks and just breathe them both in. Oh my goodness, that smell.

I fell pregnant by accident and to find out it was twins; I just couldn't get my head round it. But as the due date got closer, I started to get excited, and in the end, although I was scared of giving birth, because I had to have a C-section, it was actually very calm and ordered. I felt fine with it. My handsome boys, Terry and Simon. We were over the moon. But then it all started to go wrong. Simon developed complications. He wasn't thriving, and they found out he had a rare condition.

They did everything they could, and I prayed and prayed. But it was no good. We lost him. You think "why me?" Of course you do. But who'd have thought that just a few years later I'd lose their dad as well. It would just be the two of us. Terry and me. So, you can see why my boy is everything to me. He's all I've got.

LIFE ON PAUSE by Stephanie Stewart

Kathleen is reflecting on how it feels to live with cancer.

KATHLEEN: So, having cancer sucks! I mean, mostly it's just a lot of waiting around, not knowing what the hell is going on. I am basically home now, ALL the time! I don't get to see very many people because my immunity is shot, and I also look and feel like total crap. I don't do well being stuck inside all the time. I thrive on being around people and hustle and bustle. I'm used to being at work and being productive.

Okay, I do have my partner and kids at home with me, it could be worse, I suppose? But... I told you before, I suffer from "FOMO". All my friends and co-workers are going on without me. They're still living while I am just stuck on pause!

Oh shit! Did you get that alert too? The prime minister just announced that we have to go into a lockdown! Can life get any worse?

Pause.

Well, actually, at least now EVERYONE's life is on pause!

I don't feel so bad anymore.

DO NOT BLAME ME by Chantelle Francis

Death is on the phone and is pacing back and forth.

DEATH. So… Go to Nottingham, then Bristol and stay there? Gotcha.

Hangs up.

Oh hi. My name's Death. I always get that reaction. Don't worry, I'm not here for you.

Phone rings.

Speak. Go to London now? Okaaaay.

Hangs up. Turns to audience.

Gang violence. One of my hot providers. Stabbing. When I get close to a body, I release its soul. Pain gone. You're welcome. What? Don't look at me like that! I am the natural order of life, one of the few things that IS certain. You know, I get so much hate mail stating how "cold and uncaring" I am. Asking me "why I took them so soon"? Why? Because it's my job! That's why! And who are you calling "uncaring"? I am the MOST caring thing out here. I release people's suffering. Furthermore… People aren't yours to keep in the first place. So don't blame me because you didn't tell them you loved them when you had the chance.

Or, you let fear stop you from saying how you truly felt. That's none of my business. Fear is a different department.

I exist to teach people a valuable lesson, and that lesson is love. Without me, your perspective may never be focused on what's really important. I have to say though; the best part of the job is the family and friend reunions! I love to sing… "Reunited and it feels soooo goooood"!

Phone rings.

Speak! Yep, gotcha.

Hangs up.

Truth is, it's not my job to care about your feelings. I never said I was fair. Anyway, see you soon.

Monologues for Antagonists

IT'S KARMA by Luke Willis

Billy is responding to a threat made by his former employer.

BILLY: Don't talk to me about greed. I grafted hard at that place...zero-hour contract, no sick pay and all those false promises you made. You dangled the carrot one too many times... I'd have to be insane to want to quit this and go back to working for you. £80 million annual turnover at that place during the first year and then 6% growth each year after that. What happened to the pay increase you said I'd get? You never even gave me that permanent contract you swore you'd put me on.

Want to know what I made this morning? Three grand. I'm not glorifying it. Three grand. I'm not like you. I've got more than just myself to think about. You know when Alex was born, I'd never been so skint, desperately skint, I had to take on a second job to make up for what you WEREN'T paying me. I now know you personally had a say in that...don't even try to bullshit me you fucking leech! And you've got the nerve to accuse me of being greedy?

Admittedly, what I'm doing now is off the radar. It's not legal, but so what? Your tax dodging bosses have broken more laws than you can begin to imagine, so don't try and patronise me for wanting to give my family a better life. I know what you're doing by the way, lecturing me on responsibility and throwing around empty threats. It's pathetic. It's laughable. You couldn't end the services I've been supplying if you tried, you spineless prick, and that terrifies you. It's not greed. It's karma, mate. That's what it is. And I'm loving it!

THIS AIN'T OXFORD by Tim Bryn Smith

A senior professor, somewhat the worse for wear, has been drafted in to make a graduation speech at short notice.

PROFESSOR: Graduates, Graduates. Doesn't that sound good? Graduates of 2019, let me add my congratulations to those of the Pro Vice Chancellor and wish you every success for the future. Can I also thank Savannah for that very accomplished and inspiring student vote of thanks? I asked her just now, was she nervous about giving a speech today and she said "yes". But I'm sure you'll agree it didn't show at all, very well-done Savannah... and might I say you also look smashing. A lovely spotted dress you've got on there under your gown. Looks a bit like a nightie. With a plunging neckline.

You may not know, but I was kindly asked to fill in and close today's graduation ceremony on behalf of the Rt. Hon. Dame Irene Fitzwallace. Sadly, she couldn't make it. And, frankly, I can't blame her. I suppose once they make you a Right Honourable Dame, you might as well hang up your boots.

Slight hiccup. Sways a little. Looks to colleagues. Shrugs. Ponders. Smirks.

Where was I? Oh yes, can I also thank Mike, our alumnus today, for his rousing speech, which has certainly given you a bit of an insight into what life is like at Edgestow University.

Mimes guzzling a pint, and wobbles head between two imaginary breasts.

Go Tigers! Raaar! I came into university life for moments like this, when we get to celebrate the success of people who are about to go out and make the world a better place...if you ever get to pay off those loans...but seriously, I'm very proud to be here closing this graduation ceremony. If they had given me the vice-chancellor job in the first place…like they should have done…it would have been me here anyway. But then, how does one compete with a Dame? Especially a rich one who's also married to the Pro Chancellor. Maybe I should ask him? He's sat just there. What do you reckon Bob? Was it a mistake hiring the wife? Hmmmm... No, it's okay. I'm just wrapping up.

Turns page.

Aim for the stars, kids. You might just reach the roof tops. Providing you have husbands in high places to give you the old leg up. Or leg over. LOL. Mind he doesn't put his hand anywhere though. Where it shouldn't be. Like the crotch or breast area. Don't want a repeat of the "Lauren Salter Incident" from '96 do we Bob? Let that one slip. Is this being live streamed? Yes? Oops. Seriously though guys. Enjoy your success, it could be where some of you peak. I now declare this graduation ceremony closed.

Leaves.

Right, time for some more free Cava. It's not real Champers, by the way! This ain't Oxford!

LUCIFER CALLING by Melanie Kirkbyshire

Lucifer is on the phone to God.

LUCIFER: Ay-up. Lucifer here. You really think you're the shit, don't you, but may I remind you of the great plague of 1665-1666? One of mine I think you'll find, so I wouldn't get over-confident about all these pandemic shenanigans if I were you.

I've given you some excellent opportunities over the years to get the "end" off to an exquisitely bloody start; the Gulf War, 9-11, that Panama crisis thing and need I remind you of the Second World War? Look at how that turned out? A bit of a draw on both sides really.

You know what though? Sometimes I don't know why we bother. People are doing a pretty good job of making a mess of it all on their own. Do they really need any extra help? Did you see in the news last week? They put drunk sailors in charge of nuclear submarines, and do I need to mention global warming? They managed that all by themselves.

I'm beginning to wonder if I am really cut out for this job. It's exhausting thinking of new ways of getting humans to tarnish their souls and, it must be said, it is getting crowded down here. I am fast running out of new ways to torture corrupt police officers and politicians. I preferred it in the good old days when it was all murderers and adulterers. You know what? Sometimes I don't even bother torturing them at all. Sometimes I think existing in this universe is torment enough.

You know what I always wanted to do? Train huskies and learn how to do the foxtrot properly. Maybe I'll do that. That would make you buck your ideas up, wouldn't it? Think how full heaven would be if I put my feet up for a bit. So, sort the pandemic out, mate. You can do better than this.

I'LL SCREAM by Becki Lloyd

Lily is mentally unstable and trying to convince her ex-partner Tom to love her again.

LILY: If you don't open the door, I'll scream. Just let me in, we can just talk about this. No pressure, just a chat. Okay, well I'm going to sit here until you come to your senses.

Do you remember that Sunday afternoon last year when we went for a picnic? It was so hot and clammy but the breeze was just right…a warm breeze…anyway, remember you'd bought those cheese biscuits but forgotten the cheese, so we ate them anyway, and they were so dry? And we only had prosecco which made it even worse, like fizzy biscuit mouth? Remember how much we laughed? I think that's the most I've ever laughed.

We could get back to that. We could laugh again. I found myself in happiness with you. I promise I will never do anything to hurt you ever again. I'll be perfect, I'll be everything you want me to be. I'll never hurt myself again, I'll do that for you. You'll love me, I promise. You have to believe me; I can't live without you.

I've already told my therapist that we're having this conversation, but how am I supposed to do that if you won't open the door?

FAKE KNIVES by Danny Kendall

Josh is still wide awake. He can't get his lockdown antics out of his head.

JOSH: Why am I still awake? This is ridiculous! It's not like I have a particularly stressful day tomorrow. Or even had a busy day today. Like most people in this country of COVID, I haven't had a busy day in months. So, you do what you can to keep busy.

I recently scared off some muggers with a fake prop knife. My proudest moment! It's all part of my own personal "give-something-back" crusade.

I didn't sleep at all that night. I was buzzing. In the moment I was screaming in my best macho voice "HEY, HEY, GET AWAY FROM HIM". I don't remember reaching for the knife, must've been subconscious. It was enough to make the scumbag run away crying "FUUUCK", but not enough to stop the old man dying of a heart attack.

Ah well. I've upped my game now. Muggers beware! Since then, I've realised it's a lot more effective with an actual knife.

THIS CHARMING MAN by Julia Glancy

Lila is carefully watching the back of her husband as he makes himself a sandwich.

LILA: Sometimes I feel like killing him would be the best option. Just sticking a knife in his back or hitting him with a frying pan. Don't judge me, it wasn't always like that… Once he was this charming young man who gave me flowers and made me laugh so much. Yes. He used to make me laugh...

Small ceremony in the village church and a loud wedding reception with way too many drunk relatives. Sweet, short honeymoon in Jersey... All I can remember is the cold sea and stars; every night we would sit together cuddling and watch them. After that it went way too fast; first child, second, and the third, we barely saw each other. How busy we were! My cooking club, his whisky and cigar evenings, my volunteering at the dog shelter, his hunting trips, my Spanish lessons, his never-ending carousel of young lovers… Normal family life, you would say. Yes, it was…

And then one night I went down to the garage and saw a vision in my mind's eye. It was a vision of the floor covered in blood and that look on his face. He was happy, or so I want to believe…and I can make that happen. So here I am standing behind his back choosing between knife and pan. Shall I?

SO CALLED SUCCESSFUL PEOPLE by Conor Williams

Shawn is speaking to his former boss who has come to the hospital to visit him.

SHAWN: I suppose you've come here seeking some kind of an apology, or justification, for what I did? Well, you're not gonna like this. I detest so called successful people like you. And no, it's not because I want what you have. It's just that I hate that you have it.

Do you not think I would've stolen your car if I were envious? Yours was the 11th I burnt, by the way. I know you've probably come to say "why my house though? That was a step too far!" Or "you don't know me or how hard I've worked for this". They all love to psychoanalyse me in here. "Bitter sociopath" is the current label. And then self-proclaimed victims like yourself come to tell me I've never amounted to anything and question why I punish those who have achieved something.

Do you think your education and privileged upbringing is down to your own hard work? Because that's what's helped you pay for the material possessions you own.

They say only the wealthy can redress the balance between rich and poor and give opportunities to those who have none, essentially because they're the only ones who can afford it. Only thing though, they're very good at turning their eyes away from their social responsibilities.

That's where I come in. Don't think of me as spiteful. Think of me as your conscience. A helpful reminder that all of us can have our stuff taken from us in a matter of seconds… You're welcome.

REVENGE by Ray Simpson

A blood-soaked Tommy stands before a man tied to a chair.

TOMMY. Well, here we are, just you, me, and the cockroaches. Did you honestly think I wouldn't pursue you?

Pause.

Did you think it was a just a joke?

Pause.

Well, you got that wrong then didn't ya? You got sloppy.

Noticing the puddle beneath him.

Sniff sniff. Oh dear…have you had a little accident?

Pause.

Anyway, don't you worry about your missus and your two little sprogs, I'll make sure that they are provided for, since they are blameless in all this shit. Oh yeah, I know all about them, I even know all about your pet mongrel…Tyson.

Pause.

And I will make sure that they never, ever, find out what a fucking evil bastard you are. And the terrible things you did.

Pause.

This is for Angie.

He slits the man's throat.

JONNY ONE-BALL by Aaron Murray

Terry is at a dinner party, recounting the time his friend Tom got beaten up.

TERRY: Remember "Jonny One-Ball"? Tom and I must have been about 13 or 14. We hadn't been mates that long. Because, basically, in the first year I thought he was a bit of a twat. But then he let me copy his answers in Mr Samuel's maths test and I thought he was alright after that.

Pause.

We were always on the park playing one-man Wembley or down the crescent playing "curbee". Anyway, this one time, we were playing "wallee" in the old doctor's car park, there was broken glass everywhere and this lad "Jonny One-Ball" shows up. Usually when Jonny One-Ball rocked up, someone got their head kicked in. He said "what are you bellends doing?" Now usually, this was followed up by us with a shy "not a lot". But for some reason Tom must have been feeling a bit brave…

Pause.

Probably that bottle of 20/20 you nicked from Patel's, eh Tom? And very calmly he said... "just warming our wrists up, before we go finger your mum".

Pause.

Seriously. Every bit of air left my lungs. But poor old Tommy melted, didn't you mate! His face literally collapsed with fear. We never ran so fast! You could have done with them legs at Forest mate! What happened to that pace of yours?

Pause.

And then… Jonny One-Ball's big brother caught us outside the shop and gave us a proper pasting.

Pause.

They were the days, hey mate?

WASTE MAN by Tim Bryn Smith

Tom stands in front of a group of men in his local pub.

TOM. You've never said a true word in your entire life. You're full of it. But you need to understand. This is who I am. I'm not that goofy little kid in the picture anymore, holding the man of the match award. I'm sorry, but you need to hear this, Dad.

You wanna know why you couldn't find me all them months? It's because I got caught stealing an electric toothbrush in King's Lynn and spent three months in prison. I've messed up every job I've had since I left school. And you wanna know whose fault it is? It's yours, Dad. That's right. I'm sorry, but it's about time you heard it.

Pause.

I was walking down six flights of stairs at work today, holding a tray full of tea and coffee. And suddenly I stopped. I stopped in the middle of this massive staircase, holding all these boiling hot drinks. And I just stared out the window. At the blue sky and all these little fluffy clouds. Loads of them, stretching all the way up. And it reminded me of the few things that actually matter to me. Like feeling the sun on my back. Or just sitting, having a smoke. Being free.

When I looked back down at the teas, I thought to myself, what am I doing here? Why am I sucking up to this bunch of scoffing wankers? Why am I trying to become what I don't actually want to be?

I know I'm not a leader of men. And sorry to break it to you Dad, but neither are you. You're just an odd job man, who spends all his time in this pub, with the rest of these wastemen. Sorry gents. But it's true.

And me? Well. I guess I'm just like you, Dad. But I'm okay with that. I'll see you around.

SMALL DOG SYNDROME by Seb Sullivan

Rover sits in his basket.

ROVER. You weren't expecting that, were you? You didn't think I'd draw blood, did you? Since we met, all I've done is love you, care for you, protect you and keep you safe from harm. I'm always affectionate when you need me to be. Because we all need a cuddle from time to time.

But what do I get in return? You patronise me, feminise me, make me wear weird, stupid outfits. You stick cameras in my face 24/7 and degrade me across social media platforms. It may be in the panoptic society, but even the inmates in Bentham's Prison can take a shit in peace.

I'm not one of your idiotic friends in their strange shoes, whose only concern seems to be their eyebrows. And as much as you try, you can't force friendships. Take that dreadful meet-up in that crappy café with those ugly pink people. How many times have I told you? I don't want to play with Baxter! He's a cunt!

Anytime I try and say something sensible or constructive, I am wilfully ignored or fobbed off. I'm a fucking killing machine. I'm a warrior. I was selectively bred to hunt and kill. Not sit in a café listening to twerps gawp about "marketing" and "soft launches". When civilisation ends, I will throw off these shackles, hunt my own food, shit where I like and hump who I want.

Pause.

There's a storm coming, and the next time your poncey boyfriend comes round, I'm going to gleefully lick my balls and remind him that I'm considerably better hung.

FIRST TIMER by Samantha Badman

Tony is anxiously talking to a younger woman.

TONY: I'm a bit nervous. It's my first time, you see. I couldn't believe it when you came over to me at the bar. No-one ever comes over to me at the bar, or anywhere else for that matter. So, it was a surprise is what I'm saying. Oh, no, a pleasant surprise of course. A pleasant surprise. Sorry, I'm babbling. Like I said I'm rather nervous. First time.

Anyway, I'm sorry if I made you uncomfortable, I didn't mean to reveal as much. It must've seemed like I was stalking you. I wasn't. Well, I suppose I was in a way. I mean who wouldn't want to see as much of you as possible? Sorry. That sounds creepy.

Look. What I meant to say was, thank you. Thank you for talking to me. Thank you for being nice to me even after I "stalked" you. I've been a bit busy lately…work…you know how it is. Things to do, people to…yeah well, I probably shouldn't talk about my work. Not that it's forbidden or anything, I'm not a spy… "Hi, I'm Bond, James Bond, licensed to kill." No, I don't work for MI5 or 6 or anything. It's just that it's complicated, you know? I try to explain, but people just get riled up, so I've sort of stopped talking about it. And as I said, with a face like this, people tend not to come talk to me...

Right, I'm erm, feeling a bit calmer now, so I think I'm ready if you are?

You only lose your virginity once, right? I'm going to remove the gag now, so don't scream, okay?

Everyday Conflict

TALKING OF VEGAN BROWNIES... by Chantelle Lee

It's lunchtime and Jess is at work, responding to a colleague, Florence, who has just told a joke.

JESS: You know, that's not even the slightest bit funny! You know what's a joke? Me resisting the urge to rip your head off! You see Florence, I'm just sat here with my work friends, trying to enjoy my lunch, and all I can hear is your voice. Your irritating, bellowing, thunderous voice. At the office, when I go outside for a break, at lunchtime...jeez! I can even hear you in my dreams. There is no escape from you, your silly jokes, and your pointless chit chat. You think that it's what we all need in the office and that everyone appreciates it...well, they don't, they just find it really annoying.

I don't care that you go jogging twice a week and you feel all the better for it. I don't care about your vegan brownies that you bring into work...because, frankly, they taste absolutely revolting. And I don't want to go to your Saturday night movie nights either.

Also, would it hurt you to answer the phone once in a while, as it is - well, you know - your job? You just let that thing ring and ring... How do you do it? And you always manage to stay happy and chirpy at work...it's sickening!

Don't you ever get fed up? Because I do. You try and cheer us up with your jokes, but it doesn't work, Florence. It doesn't work and I'm afraid nothing will anymore. I wish I knew how to find something funny. Maybe I've forgotten how to laugh. I want to laugh at something, anything. It's this place, it sucks the life out of everything...but not you, you stand resilient against it all. So, I'm sorry Florence, but it's not funny, none of this is funny...the fact that I can't find anything funny is not funny.

Pause.

So, fuck it, let's have a movie night at yours on Saturday.

THE FATAL TWIN WIND UP By Nic Heeson

Patrick and Paul are twins. Paul's housemate is calling Patrick because he's concerned about Paul.

PATRICK: What's this all about? It's Paul, isn't it? I thought we sorted this all out yesterday. He was going on about calling the police if I didn't pay him back the five grand, but he knows I'm good for it.

We're always winding each other up. He punctured my tyre the other week, bet he didn't mention that! Made me late for work, my students thought I'd bailed!

I got him back last night, while I was round there. Didn't plan it, it just came to me. Thought I'd pop a few sleeping pills in his drink. It's all kosher! I'm struggling with insomnia at the minute. Left him sleeping like a baby. He's slept through his alarm, ruined his day and then realised I must have done it. Then he's rung you up. Payback time.

So, sorry for wasting your time, but it was just a few pills, no harm! It was just two, I swear. I remember tipping them out onto the counter and one dropped onto the floor, so I picked it up and then… Or were there three on the counter and one dropped on the floor? Mind's a bit cloudy. We'd had two bottles of wine beforehand. It's all fine though, right? I mean, he rang you, he's okay? Shit, please tell me he's okay. Twins are supposed to sense something bad, right?

ANGRY GIANT IN AN A-CUP by Lucy Wakefield

Lauren queues for coffee with her friend Tina.

LAUREN: Whoever said growing up was "sexy"? I mean, seriously, it's just one giant planet of "nope". And talking of planets, my arse is the size of one. And my nose. And my cheeks! Tina, I basically have a moon for a face. I envy the girls who got to "The Golden Gate" and came out looking like…like these angels. Puberty is a battleground, strewn with periods, acne, boobs…

To the barista. Two milky ones please. Yeah lattes. Thank you.

I mean you're bloody blessed with those humungous…

To the barista. Bakewell tarts. Two please. Thank you.

"Angry giant in an A-cup" they called me at school. Don't get me wrong, I don't mind being an A-cup, I never really wanted those underwired devils holding up my mammaries to the world. But for Christ's sake, I could connect my spotty-piss-puss-busters to form a galactic constellation. "Hey boys! Why stargaze when you can locate Orion's Belt on my forehead!" And don't even get me started on periods. No girl wants to wake up to a bed like a butcher's slab. And I'd be wracked with guilt. Emotions everywhere.

I know I'll never look like you. But hey, don't mind me. Maybe Mum will listen to me and my weird teenage puberty ramblings… Anyway…

To the barista. Keep the change. Thank you.

LABELS by Angela Duignan

Liz is fed up of being questioned about her sexual choices. She's defending herself to her sister.

LIZ: Because I want to… I just do. I like it, I feel good for it, I'm a nicer person sometimes because of it… I'm sick of being made to feel guilty about it. I'm sick of feeling guilty. I'm not hurting anyone. Being celibate is my business, my choice and I think it's okay. I'm okay. I'm okay, aren't I? I can stop if I wanted to, but I don't want to. The counsellor labelled me "asexual". She can label me what she likes, doesn't mean I'm going to conform.

One day I might feel differently. One day I might want a partner again, but it's up to me, isn't it? I'm so fed up with fucking "society" saying it's wrong. What's actually wrong right now with me choosing how to live my own life and taking the time I need to make decisions that affect me? Tell me!

You see, if "the only person I'm hurting is myself" - so every fucker says - then I'm quite happy. Then I don't see a problem. The problem is not mine, it's fucking society's. And you…you're making it your problem. Stop it. Stop making it yours and perhaps, just for a second, ask yourself if this is even a problem at all.

MY REGRET by Dayo Oye

Shane is in the middle of a heated argument.

SHANE. No, you need to listen to me! I'm not saying I have the biggest problems in the world, but I have issues that I need to deal with. Things I regret.

We did stupid things, we were kids. How was I supposed to keep an eye on him? If anyone should be held responsible, it's you. You are the one responsible. I should be holding you responsible. It was you that stopped us. I wanted to be there for him, but you said no. Why would you say no? He needed our support and you just…

Pause.

You will never understand how I felt. He asked me why you weren't there. Why his family wasn't there. We made him go through it alone. Can you imagine how I felt when they attacked him? Knowing that he was unconscious, lifeless in some bed somewhere.

I couldn't sleep. There was so much going through my head. And you are going to come in here and put the blame on me? Maybe it should have been me. Maybe that would have put your mind at ease.

I have nothing left to say to you.

LOVER by Kimberley Dolman

Roxy sits in a café gazing at the man sitting opposite her.

ROXY: Another day spent gazing at you, admiring your beauty. Your eyes captivate me, your smile blinds me, and your body tempts me. There isn't a star that shines brighter than you. No song can move me like you do. Nothing touches you, nothing fazes you, and I should know.

In recent months, I've been chasing you, politely pursuing you, but all in vain. I'm beyond that now. I'm beyond help now. Now I sniff your clothes, steal your things and sneak into your bed when I feel alone. It's the only way I can get close to you since she arrived on the scene.

You give your smiles so freely to her, but she doesn't know you like I do. Do you not hear how my heart beats for you? Do you not see how I am the only one worthy of you? She doesn't understand you like I do. She doesn't love you like I do. I would kill for you. I have killed for you. You will find out soon and then, finally, you'll notice me.

THE ARTS by Lucy Moon

Sophie is having an argument with her friend Ruth, who has confessed she votes Tory.

SOPHIE: You're actually in agreement with Sunak, Ruth? You're telling me you think the arts are pointless, a waste of everyone's time? Well, I disagree. I know, I know, you're not in the government...but you're here, Ruth. You're here right now. I mean, what do they know about the arts? The government?

They think the arts are "low skilled", the support package they sent out was not enough and the reply to my letter, the one I sent to my local MP, just repeated past events. "Go to work, don't go to work. Work from home if you can, but don't go to work." I mean, I wish he would just make up his mind! Come on.

They say they're doing the best they can to save jobs but are they actually considering the public? The arts have helped so many people fight their personal demons...including me. They give a voice to those who struggle to speak up.

It's not that I'm angry with you for supporting a movement that stifles creativity, Ruth. You're an adult. You make your own decisions. I'm just disappointed. I wonder if you spent a month with no TV, no music, no radio, no books and nothing pretty or thought-provoking to look at, you'd feel the same?

THE WAVE by Ashley Kingham

A surfer faces a crisis over his professional future.

SURFER. When you're out there, there's no stress, no worries. You're just completely in the moment.

I remember my dad got me my first board when I was seven and we must have spent thousands of hours out there. I could've had the worst day at school but as soon as I'd caught that first wave I'd feel on top of the world, I could do anything. I guess I still spend so much time out there because it's really the only way I know that I can still feel connected to him.

I went down to the beach early on Saturday to try and avoid all the tourists. I'd been waiting to surf all week and was just so stoked to get on a wave that I didn't even notice there was a little kid there, just paddling out.

By the time I'd seen him and bailed off my board it was too late. The fins must have caught him in the face coz when I pulled him onto the beach, all around his eye was just gushing with blood. Then the lifeguards bolted over, pushed me out the way, and he got rushed to hospital.

I came back to the beach later that day and asked the lifeguard on duty "you heard anything about that kid?" and she said, "well he's never going to see out of that eye again".

So now, because of me, a little kid has had his life ruined, and the only thing left that really mattered to me…is tainted. Forever.

Pause.

So, what am I supposed to do now?

HIDE THE SHARK by David Hoare

Keith has just finished setting up a webcam. He assumes an aggressive stance and stares into the camera.

KEITH. My name is Keith Heptonstall and I am a security and self-defence advisor. My background is ex-army…cadets.

I've just completed an online martial arts course. I'm a "virtual" blackbelt. Some might say that I'm a lethal weapon. Okay?

I've developed my own style of martial arts using the "Crouching Beaver" (*forms giant teeth with his left hand*) and "Hidden Shark" (*forms a fin on his head with his right hand*) technique.

And I'm going to teach you how to use this technique, normally used by actors to tap into past life experiences, to portray different states of emotion. Yes, by using the methods of Stanislavski and Meisner to recall childhood trauma, I can help you convert feelings into pure fucking violence against an opponent or assailant. Okay…

Pause.

I'll give you a scenario.

Pause.

You're in bed and you hear a noise downstairs. *Pulls scared face.* It's a break-in. Okay?

Pause.

The first thing you think, is… *Pulls vicious face.* Wrong house pal.

Whispering and tip toeing. You go downstairs. And there he is… *Suddenly jumping up and striking an aggressive pose*. Let's go!

Turns into a screaming child. "Haaaaa! Haaaaaaaaaaa! You're not my real dad!"

In own voice. "Hide the Beaver, Release the Shark."

Turns back into screaming child. "You're just my weekend daddy…Stop telling me what to do…Nooo...Mr Clark I don't want to do PE!"

In own voice. "Hide the Shark, Release the Beaver. Hide the Shark. Hide the Shark."

Okay. Okay… I hope that can be of good use to you.

Pause.

Next week, I'll teach you how to make a bomb out of a rabbit.

FOLK LAW by Tim Bryn Smith

A Polish man sits on a park bench.

HIRED GUN. A thousand years ago, or maybe more, there lived three brothers: Lech, Czech, and Rus. For many years they had been content in their little village, but as families grew, they needed more room to live. The brothers decided to travel in different directions to make a new home.

Lech, Czech, and Rus travelled for many days. They rode their horses over mountains and rivers, through forests and wild country where there were no people to be found anywhere, not a town or village. On the crest of a mountain top, they separated, each going in a different direction. Czech went left, Rus to the right and Lech straight ahead, down the mountain and across vast plains.

Lech travelled for many, many years. He was so tired. Almost dying. And then Lech saw a most majestic sight. He had come to a place where a beautiful meadow surrounded a small but very beautiful lake. And at the edge of the meadow, a great eagle flew over his head. It flew around in great swooping circles, then perched on its nest, high on a black rock. Lech stared in awe at this wondrous sight. And as the eagle spread its wings and soared into the heavens again, a ray of sunshine from the red setting sun fell on the eagle's wings, so as to appear tipped with shining gold. The rest of the bird was the purest white. "Here is where we will stay!" declared Lech. "This is our new land, and this is the place we will call home”.

Pause.

I think I go back to my country. I miss my family. I miss countryside. I miss Baltic Sea. Mountains. Good beer. Good wine. Bigos. Pierogi. Schabowy. My beautiful Gabriela.

Pause.

Brexit. You want me out of UK? It’s okay. I go. There’s too many lies here anyway. Too many secrets.

I need a drink.

Talking to my Therapist

NAKED FOR THE FIRST TIME by Claire Waterall

Polly is talking to her therapist.

POLLY: I flashed my tits to the window cleaner this morning. I don't know what came over me. One minute I'm in the bedroom putting away my clean undies and the next thing I know, I'm standing at the window with my dressing gown open revealing my 34DDs. Okay. 32Bs.

The window cleaner (or SpongeBob Dave as I like to call him) didn't notice at first. He was going about his business, whistling away and then he glanced up. Our eyes met and I stood there, still as a statue. My heart beating so hard I thought it would burst out of my chest and splatter on the net curtains. At first, I thought he might scream or laugh, but he just gave me a sad smile and went down his ladder.

The thing is, no one has ever seen me naked before. I've never been kissed. Never been desired. Never had a boyfriend, never had any real friends either. It's just been me and my mum for as long as I can remember.

Mum passed away last week. Died in her sleep. I was bringing her up a cup of tea and there she was. She looked peaceful. All those years she'd abused her body yet here she was, so still, with not a mark on her face. As I looked at her a wave of relief flooded my body. At last, I was free. I think that's why I did what I did this morning even though I know it was fucked up. I wanted to feel alive. I wanted to finally be seen.

KILLJOY By Adrianna Liu

Lana is explaining to her therapist why she is on the anger management course.

LANA: I know they say that loving yourself is the greatest love of all, but Brock takes it to new heights. He walks around like he is a gift to the Earth and the worst thing is, people like him. He relentlessly tells us "funny" anecdotes of his wild youthful days, especially while he was doing a year abroad in Harvard. He talks about it so much I don't think there's a single person in the office who doesn't know he studied there. Sometimes I'll reluctantly fake a chuckle, so people don't think I'm a killjoy, and I hate myself for it.

When he sees me in the office, he'll go "Smile! You're not at a funeral!" Every time he says it, I want to slam his head against the desk for having the audacity to tell me what to do with my face, but I don't. It's not professional.

He also does this thing, where he offers to help his colleagues with their work, particularly the female ones, even though we don't ask for it. He proceeds to lean in so close, you can smell his coffee breath. His arm will reach around the back of your chair and lightly brush his fingers against your back. I hate it, but again, I don't say anything. Stay out of trouble, I tell myself.

Then, a couple days ago, I bumped into him in the kitchen and as he goes to leave, he squeezes past me. As he does so, he lightly places his hands around my waist to move me gently to the side. Does he do this to Harry when he walks past him, I wonder? And Tom, and Gary?

It was then that I saw red. I spun around and I smacked the lights out of him. If I'm honest I don't really remember what happened, it was all a blur. My boss was…outraged. He told me that violence in the workplace was unacceptable. That's why I've been enrolled here…to work on my "anger issues". He told me I had to complete the course if I wanted to keep my job, so here I am…although I can't say I'm really sorry. If anything, I feel…incredible! You know what, fuck it. Fuck my boss, fuck the whole company and most of all fuck Brock! I'm out.

HOW TO SPICE UP YOUR LOVE LIFE by Tammy Heath

Tracey is unimpressed with Gary's interpretation of what their couples therapist advised them to do to spice up their love life.

TRACEY: Bloody hell Gary, you've ripped my dress. It's from Oasis. Cost me a friggin fortune. I mean, was that good for you Gary? Is that what gets you off? This is so typical. It's all about what works for you. Did you even think to stop and ask yourself whether, you know, I was ready down there? Or even in the friggin mood yet? Just because the bloody therapist said to "spice things up" and "be spontaneous", it does not give you the right to wham-bam-thank-you-mam me in the middle of making dinner. I was already trying to be spontaneous. I mean just look at me, Gary. I have dressed up, done my hair, put my slap on and I WAS in the middle of making us a nice meal. Look, I'm not saying that it wasn't appreciated, well I am saying that, but I get what you were trying to do.

Kev and Dawn don't have to go to therapy Gary, and they've been married longer than us, but the way he looks at her… They have deep conversations, Gary. He takes her out, he compliments her, HE's romantic, Gary. Don't look at me like that, you're not the one who has to hear about how perfect their fucking marriage is every five fucking minutes. Or how sensational their lovemaking is. Or how it goes on all night long like Lionel fucking Richie. Talk about TMI. At least, when the longest you've ever lasted is 12 minutes including foreplay, you're not going to go around shouting about your sex life. That's something, I suppose.

Oh, fuck them and fuck this therapy shit. No amount of spontaneous role-playing is gonna help us Gary, so tell you what…you go out and buy me another dress and I'll try and rescue this chicken chasseur. Maybe by the time you come home, I'll have got my mojo back…

THE CALL OF THE VOID by Tegan Rowe

Amelia confesses her paranoia and desire to let go just a little more.

AMELIA: Do you ever think about losing control? I think about it all the time. Every time I pick up, I don't know, a plate, or a mug, I imagine dropping it and watching it smash on the tiled floor. I imagine time slowing and being able to see each piece of ceramic fly into the air.

When I'm at work and I'm carrying a tray of drinks down the stairs, I always envision the moment I go full Bambi and my legs buckle beneath me. I'll tumble down the steps, coffee in my hair, baked beans down my shirt and egg quite literally on my face.

Even when losing control is supposed to be a good thing, I find myself panicking. Like...when I (*mouthed*) orgasm. I once had sex with a guy who...well I won't go into details...but let's just say I kind of ruined it when I accidentally kneed him in the jaw. And now every time I have sex, or even think about sex, I remember that moment and I imagine it happening again.

Sometimes I think about actively losing control. I mean, not on purpose, but not exactly by accident either. Sometimes I see a pensioner with a walking stick, and I imagine kicking it so that they fall over, or opening the car door as we race down the motorway at 70 miles per hour, or jumping on the train tracks at the station, just because you know you're absolutely not supposed to do that.

That's awful, isn't it? Is that normal? To feel an urge to do that? I just feel that my grip on things is...ever so tight. Perhaps I need to learn how to let go a little more.

HARSH REALITY by Laura Jane Johnson

A young woman speaks to her therapy group.

YOUNG WOMAN. The last time I went out without worrying about my mum was when I was about 18. I was going on a night out with friends and we got ready at mine. My girls helped me do my make-up and we laughed as we tried on each other's clothes and danced to Britney. God, I love Britney!

We headed into town and I can remember drinking these amazing cocktails, that had these edible little bits of glitter in them. We didn't stop dancing all night. Afterwards, I went back to my friend's house and fell asleep on her floor. It was the best night.

I got up in the morning with a huge headache and I just wanted my own bed. So I got a taxi home, which cost me a fortune. When I got home, I couldn't get in because I'd lost my bloody key. I tried to shout through the letterbox, but no one answered. I just felt that something was wrong.

So, I jumped over the side gate and I went round the back. The side door was open. When I walked in, my dad was standing there with his friend. They both just looked at me. I then walked through to the lounge and mum was there, lying on the sofa in her dressing gown. She just looked at me.

Dad then walked up to me, hugged me, and told me that she had taken an overdose.

Pause.

What the hell? I couldn't even look at her, I was so fucking angry. What a fucking selfish thing to do. I mean, how can she do that to her children? I still can't forgive her for it. What a selfish bitch.

SLEEPING WITH THE MILITARY by Gina Taylor

Suzie is talking to her therapist

SUZIE: I think the problem was lack of sleep and everything around me contributed to that; inconsiderate girls in the mess, the long hours, and not seeing daylight for days on end. Then there'd be the Harriers taking off and crashing down onto the flight deck late at night.

The worst part was the ship going astern, what the hell was with that? It would leave me literally bouncing and vibrating in my pit. Don't even get me going with how deafening it was. It's a glorified tin can, for God's sake, freezing in the winter months and like an oven in the warmer months. In the rough seas, I seriously thought we were going to tip over. Who can sleep through that?

I'm doing it again. Moaning! Look, I mean, don't get me wrong because it isn't all bad. I've made some lifelong mates and I've got some really fond memories of performing with the band for the ship's crew. As for the runs ashore and getting pissed up with the ME lads, when I never had to buy a beer, they were epic! I was getting on well with my boyfriend until recently too.

It's just now it's not great, I suppose, as we've actually split up. I ended it, over the phone. You must think I'm a right bitch, but the separation was just too much while I was away. We just argued, we got frustrated because neither of us had much to say. The sleep, the lack of sleep just destroyed me, it took away my smile. The irony is that since we broke up, I can sleep again.

FREAKING OUT by Fiona Robertson

In her therapist's consulting room, Sarah has a sudden epiphany.

SARAH. Try to calm down? You sit there, with your unruffled hair and your professional empathy, which I pay for, and think you have the right to tell me to "calm down"? Are you kidding me? Have you seen what's out there? What good are measured tones and logic when there's killing, starvation, torture, brain tumours, insane heatwaves…

Who, in the face of all of that, sleeps tight at night? What are you? Cut off at the neck? Blind? Or so numb you really believe the world is a safe, sane place? I realise now, I've been trying not to freak out when freaking out is the only honest option. I thought there was something wrong with me because I'm terrified. And you've allowed me to go on believing that. Of course you have. That's another £70 in your bank account every week.

God, I am so sick of being restrained and playing it safe when that's not what's going on here. I'm going to die. We're all going to die. What if we were honest with each other? What if we paid attention? We'd stop putting up with all this shit. There would be a revolution!

So, no. I will not try to "calm down". I've had enough of your violence dressed up as salvation. I want my aliveness back. So, I will not rein it in or pacify or placate or deny just to make you feel better. I will freak the fuck out for as long as the freak out lasts.

Monologues About Grief

A SUICIDE OF CONVENIENCE by Ben Grace

Julian is at his friend's grave.

JULIAN: If you're going to kill yourself then you should at least make sure that it's a massive inconvenience to everyone around you. I know that's not what people usually say in these situations, but I think it's best to go in the most dramatic and inconvenient way possible. Make the incident famous and give it a mythical status! That's what I say!

It gives your loved ones a better story to tell. "Oh, do you remember the gentlemen that stopped traffic on the M1 by tying his ankles to the back of the lorry before shooting a firework into his face? That was our Steve. Yes, he's dead. Very troubled young man."

You could have thought of all this when you were alive. It's not like we didn't talk about death. Instead, you did it in the most boring, convenient, and clichéd way possible.

Pause.

An overdose.

Pause.

How pedestrian. So, I don't have a choice in how I tell it. It feels real, not mythical. I can't roll my eyes or stifle a mis-timed giggle. It's not a story and you're really gone. And I'm really alone. The least you could have done was leave a mess.

IT'S ALEX BY THE WAY By Alliyah Mukri

Alex is missing her friend who was taken too soon.

ALEX: Hey, it's Alex. Again. I was thinking of you again today. I passed that church near your old house. You know the one with the smashed stained glass and rotting bench? I'm not sure why I'm calling, actually. As if you'd actually pick up. Did I say it was Alex by the way? I think I did.

I guess I've just been having a hard time this past year not seeing you. It's been tough. I left a voicemail a couple months back to tell you I lost my job. Did you get that? Well, I still haven't found one. It's kind of my own fault. I stopped turning up after you left because I couldn't bear to be there while you weren't.

It's weird working with someone every day and then one day have them up and leave. I'm sorry, I know you didn't mean it. I'm not blaming you. My parents split up too. That was probably my fault as well. I guess my heartbreak triggered theirs. I won't be able to afford my phone bill if I carry on listing everything else wrong in my life.

I don't know why I keep leaving you voicemails. I guess I'd be even more worried if you actually did pick up. I know you're not here anymore, but I love you and I miss you. Your mum can't bear to look at me. I don't blame her. I should've known you were feeling so down. I'm sorry you had to try to stop it on your own. I'm sorry I didn't get you the help that you needed and I'm sorry that I cry all night while you should be resting in peace, leaving far too many voicemails and listening to this haunting beep.

I don't think I actually can accept that you're gone and there's nothing more that I want than to be wherever you are now. Did I say it was Alex by the way? I'm not sure if… *(Phone cuts out.)*

THE FIRE WITHIN by Andrew Henry

Sean is at his Mum's grave.

SEAN: I remember seeing the beauty of the flames, brushing upon my skin. The scorching temperature rising and rising each second and the sweat flowing down my face. Hearing that scream in the house, caged by the heat... I didn't hesitate, not for a second. I rushed through the house, the smoke blinding my vision, my heart pounding, trying to follow that crying out for help, getting closer and closer. And then I saw it...a photo of him...with his new family...

As if he forgot what he did to us and how we lost everything. My hatred engulfed me then, raging with the flames, reminding me why I was there and, as I turned, he was there on the floor, helpless. Our eyes were locked on to each other. The shock on his face said it all, as if he knew his time was up. The past always comes back to haunt you... It's all over, Mum. Now you can rest in peace.

SARAH VS PIZZA by Sophie Corner

Sarah is talking to her pizza in the oven.

SARAH: Oh really? You're going to turn your back on me! After everything we've been through? I don't deserve this. I don't deserve any of this.

After a long day in the office talking to Gerald from marketing about a flopped Instagram post, and Steve from ICT about the importance of clearing cookies and who knows fucking what - what even is a fucking COOKIE? I thought... I thought for a second that you wouldn't let me down. You could be the one thing I could confide in, could depend on, but no! You had to be fucking – cheeseless!

A fucking plain ass pizza, no cheese bloody pizza, what's the concept here? Buy cheese and tomatoes separately and create your own? Oh wait. It's upside down.

She would be laughing at me so much right now... And I don't even like pizza. She was the one with the serious pizza habit. It was the one thing she really missed eating at the end. She would never have admitted that. She believed herself a woman of impeccable taste. But I knew. I tried to mash some up once and put it in her feeding tube...didn't go down well. Quite literally. And the nursing staff were livid. It mucked up her meds and made a mess everywhere. Brought a sparkle to her eye though. She appreciated it!

At the funeral, I had a bit more pizza success. Obviously, because I got catering from Domino's. Lucky it was a Tuesday 2 for 1 deal. I asked the undertaker if that discount also applied to the coffin prices... It did not.

Well, there's always next week. Let's try that again. Ashes to ashes, dust to dust, please let there be a deep pan crust. I miss you, Mum.

WHAT HAPPENED TO WARREN? by Danny Shooter

Liam tells the story of a singer's demise and how it affected him.

LIAM: The first time I saw Warren he stepped up to the microphone and roared like a lion. His voice was gravel caught in his throat. The coarse, sharp stones shaved the skin from his throat as he belted the high notes to *Child of Mine*. His voice amplified to fill the vast, empty room. Empty, save for a table of men with long beards holding up their pints.

"Waaaay," they cheered. Warren cheered back.

The second time I saw Warren he left the stage to change into his costume.

"He's eccentric," someone said.
"It's just Warren," offered someone else.
"Why can't he just be himself. Who knows? I like it."

One night I was on stage, scared and hidden behind my guitar. Warren came to see me. He asked, "Do you play any popular songs?"

I said I only play my own stuff. He invited me to perform with them, which was kind, but I was too nervous. I wished I was like Warren. He would disappear behind a veil of smoke and music as though performing to 5,000 people. He danced and screamed and forgot his words.

Then one day Warren wasn't there.

"Have you heard what happened to Warren?" That's what my dad asked me. Then an entire life reduced to a single word.

"Dead. Overdose last week. Heard it from your brother."

"Shit."

We spent a lot of time with Warren, but we never knew him. None of us did. Not really.

THE LAST GOODBYE by Hannah Sowter

Jayne tries to make sense of the last few weeks before her friend's death.

JAYNE: Well, here we are, sat here together for our final time. The thing I've learnt most from this year is that life is strange, full of hidden expectations and surprising thoughts. But the one thing that shocked me was the death of you.

Last time I saw you we were with our other friends, drinking and having fun. You complained of some aches and pains, but shrugged it off, thinking you'd come down with a bug.

When I didn't hear from you the next day I began to worry, thinking it was something I had done. I found out a week later that you'd been diagnosed with terminal cancer.

I didn't know how to respond, my mind filled with hopelessness and mourning, but I threw myself into learning how to be there for you with the little time you had left. I didn't know you'd die before we'd get to say goodbye.

With time on my hands now and you in my heart, I can't calm the irritation I feel about having to find out about your diagnosis from everyone else. And not you. I felt as though I was a bad friend. I know I sound a bit selfish, as though I'm making it about myself; but I just cared, and I wanted to be there for you.

I'm sorry for being angry. I'm not sure if my reaction is funny, dumb, or outrageous. But perhaps it simply demonstrates just how much you were loved.

GIVE ME ONE DAY by Natasha Lewis

Lisa reflects on her grief.

LISA: When he died, my life did a 180. Food doesn't taste the same anymore, music has a different rhythm, and being around people often feels...sore. I may walk straight, but inside I'm on my knees.

"At least he's in peace."

"Time is a healer."

For fuck's sake, I don't want to hear it. I just can't bear to listen to it anymore. All this love in my soul has nowhere to go. So, it fills my eyes with tears and leaves a lump in my throat. When his favourite songs play on the radio, or something comes on TV that reminds me of him, it pounds in my chest.

"Grief is the love that can't be given to the person you most want to give it to." Did someone say that once? Or did I just make that up?

"We must learn to live with one foot in the past, one foot in the now, and take our peace wherever we find it."

Actually, that wasn't too bad. Hold on...where's my pen, I better write it down before I forget. He always said I should be a writer.

On the Verge of a New Life

MARRIED AT FIRST SIGHT by Fiona Wright

Frankie is in her mid-thirties, an independent, smart, outgoing woman, who is no stranger to the world of dating. She knows what she wants and explains to her good friend Kim how it's all going.

FRANKIE: How's the dating going? Well, I've experienced just about everything from intense and possessive, to creepy and boring. There's the egotistical ones with their dick pics and the tactile ones who undress you with their eyes.

I mean, how hard is it to meet an attractive, nice, normal, kind, honest, fun, outgoing guy with nice teeth and decent shoes? Oh, and not forgetting a full head of hair! Not that I'm being bald-ist, but it doesn't really do it for me… I just want to settle down.

There was this one guy that turned up to a date who didn't look anything like his pictures; chipped tooth, pot belly and bad shoes; no effort made whatsoever. Anyway, it transpired that he had been married ten years previous, to what now is his ex-wife. At the time he had arranged to fulfil her fantasy, by having a threesome. And then she ran off with his best friend!

It's exhausting, soul destroying and like looking for a needle in a haystack. So, to answer your question - pretty shit! That is why I have applied to a TV show and I am letting a group of experts find me a husband. I'll be getting married to a complete stranger. Maybe they can get it right! Are you coming on my hen do then?

INSTANT DISMISSAL by Steph Lacey and adapted by Luke Willis

Lee wears a headset and works at a desk in "The Call Centre".

LEE. *(Talking into headset.)* Good afternoon, Lee speaking, how can I help? Yep right, I'm afraid you're through to the wrong department...No, you want extension 4... I'm unable to transfer you unfortunately. Okay, take care. Bye.

(Turns to colleague sitting close by.) Did you hear what happened to Daniel on Monday? Oh my God, seriously. Right, he's on the blower to this customer, some old woman, and she's proper laying into him! Accusing him of single-handedly putting her family in debt! Yeah! Anyway, Daniel's right pissed off at this point, so he puts the phone on mute so he can go fucking ballistic at her, calling her a "stupid old bag". Apparently, he even called her a "chicken fucker"! God knows where he got that from! Anyway, he looks down at his phone... He's not pressed the mute button, has he? She's heard the entire thing! Instant dismissal if you swear down the phone at a customer.

(Talking into headset.) Good afternoon, you're through to the Call Centre, Lee speaking, how may I help? Absolutely! I'll get that in the post to you immediately! *(Mutes customer.)* Will I fuck! *(Unmutes customer.)* Yeah, it should be with you between three to five working days. Okay, take care, Bye.

(Turning to colleague.) Tell you what. Some of these new starters. Look at 'em! Been here five minutes and already got their noses buried into the manager's arsehole. Makes me sick. Not you, you're alright. But look at her! Apparently, she's worked at three call centres in the last 18 months. Can't hold a job down can she! Fucking bitch. It's a…

(Talking into headset.) Good afternoon, you're through to the Call Centre, Lee speaking, how can I help? Sandra? I'm afraid she finished at 3:30. Of course, she's in at 10am tomorrow if you want to try then? All right, Okay, cheers, thanks, ta, bye-bye.

(Turning to colleague.) Always try and get the last "bye" in at least once a shift if you can. Just a little thing me and a few of the lads have got going here. Well, me anyway. Tell you what, that Richard's all right isn't he? The only bit of eye-candy in the office. I'd fuck him. Apparently, him and one of the temps spit-roasted one of the old accountants in the store cupboard! Honestly! Now that's a sandwich I'd like to be a slice of.

(Talking into headset.) Good afternoon, you're through to the Call Centre, Lee speaking, how can I help? Yes? *(Mutes customer.)* It's another old bag. *(Unmutes customer.)* No, no, it's Lee… Lee… Lima, Echo, Echo… Of course, could I start by taking your name please? And the first line of your address and postcode? I'm afraid I've got nothing coming up under that postcode, could you repeat that for me please? Okay, I'll

repeat that back to you, I've got November, Golf, Sixteen, Five, Double Penetration. SHIT! SHIT!

(Turning to colleague.) That's an instant dismissal.

THE REVOLTING FARMERS by Fiona Robertson

The Minister for the Environment, Food and Rural Affairs, who has been in post since the early days of Brexit, addresses their long-time political advisor.

MINISTER FOR THE ENVIRONMENT: Jeremy, back in 2016 you said the fishermen will be a problem, but the farmers have been so battered by Brussels bureaucracy that they'll be eating out of your hands. They'll be so grateful to escape the clutches of the EU, you said, they'll let you get away with anything in the negotiations. So perhaps you can advise me, Jeremy, why I am now seeing and smelling a mound of crap right outside the ministry? Actual crap, Jeremy! Seventeen tons of actual bullshit! And any second now, that crap will be smeared all over the country's newsfeeds.

How have we gone from battered, docile farmers eating out of my hands to very angry, but very photogenic farmers coming all the way from Devon in their bright red muck spreaders to fling actual shite at me? What's the point of having an advisor if his advice is so shit it results in a load of actual shit being dumped on me?

Here's what we're going to do. Get the clean-up crews, Jeremy. Invite the farmers' leaders to a meeting at 2pm, and for God's sake make sure they've showered before they come up. Set up a press conference for 3pm. And then, Jeremy, write your resignation letter. You thought I wouldn't be able to get rid of you before January, didn't you, but this situation is just too important. I'm not going to allow your incompetence to be diluted in a smorgasbord of incompetence. Let it shine, I say. And let it be punished.

THE KEEPERS OF THE LOST CAUSE by Lisa Chamberlain

Autumn 1845. Branwell Brontë, errant brother to Charlotte, Emily and Anne, discusses his present situation with his sculptor friend, Joseph Leyland.

BRONTË: Drink is my salvation. That is what my sisters fail to comprehend. Heads poring over their interminable scribblings, what know they of the pressures that beset me? They afford me no latitude…stubborn Charlotte, tempestuous Emily and pallid Anne.

Is it not clear, Joseph? I am the male of the species, the heir, the one destined for greatness, and yet I remain entrenched within a domestic gaol. But still, it amuses me to see their terror writ large. "Whatever will become of him?" This is their constant refrain.

Then there is father, the esteemed Reverend Brontë. I catch him mumbling in his sleep, wrestling with the demons of MY creation, HIS hope turned to ashes. Tell me, dear friend, what see you when you look upon this countenance? The unruly hair, the patched-up spectacles, the obscene nose? Hardly providential, I admit… Yet she loves me. Mrs Robinson, my lodestar. We will be married, of that I am certain. She. Believes. In. Me.

And so, for her sake, and for father's, I shall press on, until my novel is complete and the name of Branwell Brontë is lauded high and low. The ultimate in literary offering from the Brontë colossus!

CORPORATE FIZZ by Clare Wood

Joanne is a 46-year-old single mum, who's just been sacked by the company at which she's worked for 12 years.

JOANNE: So, my life changed today. I'm not sure how I feel about it. A little bit of a kick in the teeth, but also a lot of fear. 12 years I've given to that company, 12 years of selling fizzy pop in order to line the pockets of the corporate bellends; and they ditched me despite the month's overtime I put into the rebranding launch.

Actually, that sits really uncomfortably with me. I never wanted to play their game. It's just not me. But I kept doing it, selling my soul, and screwing people over in order to pay the mortgage and go away on holiday with my daughter a couple of times a year.

You know what? This is a good thing. I'm gonna have to get myself organised. I'll need to go shopping. I need a new car, and a phone, and a laptop. What shall I do? It's sort of exciting isn't it, finishing that chapter that I know I had been dragging out for far too long? Bye, bye bellends. Hello new me!

RESPONSIBILITIES by Tim Bryn Smith

Terry is with friends.

TERRY: Thursday nights at Rock City were brilliant. It was student night, so there was less grebs knocking about than usual. Didn't have to worry about "fertility cycles" and mercury in my fish back then. Just had to make sure I had a fiver left in my skyrocket for Victoria Kebabs on the way home. Course, that's if I didn't pull. I don't mean to sound like a prick, but I didn't do too badly back in them days, on the old pulling front.

Pause.

Man, I'd not had a BIG night out for some time. And the last time I did, I woke up in the Arboretum with a shitting slug on my face. Can't remember much about that night to be honest, but I know I wasn't alone.

Pause.

Oh, don't get me wrong. Bea and I are happy. She's happy. I'm happy. We're "happy". But life is stressful sometimes. Work's stressful. Parents are stressful. Knowing the right thing to do all the time is stressful. No one warns you that when you hit your 30s life is one hairy, sweaty, dangling pair of bollocks!

Pause.

You just got to be the big man and take responsibility for whatever life throws at you.

A NEW CHAPTER by Oliver Topping

Ed gives a speech to his family during a graduation celebration.

ED: Every morning for as long as I can remember I've woken up with no motivation or desire at all. But I've done what I had to do because all I've wanted to do is to make you proud.

I'm sorry. I want to see the world. And not from an office window, or from behind a countless pile of 10-Q's. I want to help people, help people who actually need my help, not clients of Goldman Sachs.

It's time for me to do what I think I need to do.

How am I going to do that? I don't know, but this is the time to find out, isn't it? Not after I've lost every scrap of individuality from trying to climb the corporate ladder. This is the start of a new chapter, one I'm going to write for myself.

BROADCASTING TO THE ENEMY by Jazmin Anthony

Temi is at her house trying to take photos for her Instagram account. She is visibly frustrated with herself as she needs the photos up before peak "liking" time but can't seem to find the right angles or lighting. She runs in screaming with excitement and shaking her phone.

TEMI: Hey there, this is Temi and I just want to say thank you to all my fans who have made this moment in my life possible. Also, a big thank you to all my enemies…Tenemies…who have kept me trending every single goddamn week, this one's for you huns. I can't believe it, I really can't. I've finally hit one million followers on Insta. Honestly, this is a lifelong dream and I cannot WAIT to…

Temi sees a notification pop up on her phone screen. The local newspaper has picked up the latest story on her being dropped from one of the UK's biggest fashion hosiery brands – Bibi's Boutique. The phone is still recording.

No no no no no this can't be right. Are you actually joking me? How the hell did I just get dropped from Bibi Boutique's hosiery campaign? I thought the whole idea was to promote female empowerment. Oh, c'mon, surely the caption of my post "hos before bros" totally represents that. Noooooo! They're leaving me. I'm going to have no followers at this rate. Come back you faceless, vacuous, soulless GHOULS!

I started this channel to give myself a sense of purpose since my mum died. I just wanted to escape to a reality where I wasn't the weird unpopular girl in school. Now look at me, trapped in a world of social media that's even worse. My whole life is exposed and lived through this lens of a completely distorted reality. It's all fake and it's physically and mentally draining. No one can prepare you for the amount of hate messages you receive. Every tiny flaw I have is magnified and every opinion I share is scrutinized. I just...I don't know if I can do it anymore.

Temi hears her phone buzz and light up next to her on the desk.

No way has Cosmo magazine just picked up the article about me being dropped by Bibi's Boutique! Oh my god and I've just gained 1,000 more followers in that time! Oh shit. I'm live. Did I just broadcast all of that?

THE POLITICAL POWER OF SPINACH By Emily Radford

Alice is the new advisor to the Cabinet Minister. She knows she needs to signal to him that something's wrong during his keynote speech, but she's terrified.

ALICE: Should I let him know or not? On the one hand, I could just say it quickly and then it'll be over with. The conversation can move on. Everything will be forgotten about. Or, on the other hand, he might take it the wrong way and get upset. And when he gets upset, he can wipe 10% off a country's GDP! Oh God. I can't decide.

It's kind of grossing me out a little now. But yet, at the same time, I can't stop myself from looking at it. Should I look into his eyes and smile to signal to him that he's doing great? Or point at his mouth and indicate that there's a problem? Oh, I hope I'm not making it obvious... He definitely knows by now that I'm not listening to what he's saying. Concentrate girl, come on. He's looking at me for a response. This is just getting worse.

When I took on the role of being his PA a week ago, I thought I'd fall down on memorising the statistics, not have a meltdown about telling him he appears to have a field of spinach between his teeth during his keynote speech; a pet hate of the PM who's watching. This could bugger up his promotion. And mine! Wait, he's looking in the mirror across the room. Oh, I think he's seen it. Yes! He has seen it and he's taking it out! Eeeeeeew. And he's laughing. Laugh back. Okay, good.

It's okay girl, you've still got a job, just play it cool. Give him a thumbs up.

THE CHOICE by CC Anderson

Natalie confronts the man who broke her heart.

NATALIE: I didn't think that after so long you would still have the same effect on me. But you do. It's not something I can help. The thing that we had - framed by the past - was beauty itself. How lucky we were to experience it. But don't get the wrong idea. Don't look at me like that, and please don't come any closer.

To this day I truly feel like we could have made it work. Yes, I chose my career, but I also chose you! You're the one who gave me an ultimatum, which was totally unfair because I told you about my career ambitions when we first started dating. I was committed to our relationship, but I wasn't about to throw all of my hard work away for you.

If it were the other way around, nobody would think it unusual for me to follow you and be patient! But, because I'm a woman, I'm expected to drop all my dreams, goals and desires because a man has chosen me!

People had you coined as some saint and me as the villain because I chose my acting career! Yet you moved on so quick, as if I didn't mean shit to you! Your little girl must be what, three now huh?

I remember learning that you were expecting a baby, a month after we broke up. Everything fell apart. I wasn't being cast for roles, people were so angry with me for destroying our relationship and letting go of a "good man".

But you know me, I wasn't built to break. I channelled that energy and worked my ass off! Life is looking brighter with a new lead role in a Hollywood feature film, and you see that guy over there? Yes him, he's my fiancé.

THE FIRST CUT by Elise Cummings

Pippa is on the phone to John, while she studies her reflection in the mirror.

PIPPA: John, this will have to be the last time. I can't do this anymore. I just feel so guilty thinking about Nicky. He's going to notice that I've not been around as much. I can't risk him finding out…or worse …someone else telling him. That nosy cow Delilah almost spotted me leaving yours the other day. She practically posts her every bowel movement on Facebook, so she's bound to let it slip if we're not careful.

No! Don't be daft, of course you haven't done anything wrong! You're amazing. Listen, since I've been seeing you, I've felt like a new woman. My friends say I look years younger. You've transformed me…and the way you use your hands...you're like a wizard! It's just Nicky and I, we have so much history and ten years is no small thing you know? He's a very sensitive soul and this would just crush him.

It's not that he's a bad person, but just over the years it feels like he stopped listening to what I really wanted. Unlike you. You know exactly how to satisfy me. I come away from you feeling so great about myself. But it's not fair on Nicky. This isn't easy for me. Do you think I want this? Oh, don't sigh at me like that John. I can't bear it. Look, okay, fine. Book me in for a cut and blow dry for a week on Wednesday. But this is the last time. I mean it.

Unlucky in Love

BIG CREEPY ROMANTIC GESTURES by Emma Wighton

Grace is in the kitchen surrounded by peonies.

GRACE: James loves me…or so he says! But I can't help but feel irritated by the same routine every damn time I see him. He drives round to pick me up from home. He stays in the car when he reaches my house because "fuck saying hi to my parents…he's not dating them!" We buy pizzas from Tesco. We go to his. We cook the pizzas. Then we watch a crap film until I fall asleep…at which point he shakes me awake and complains "YOU'RE NOT WATCHING IT"!

No, James. I'm not watching it because: a) It's shite and b) I'M FUCKING TIRED!

He then turns off shite film and, despite my evident exhaustion from life in general, decides it's an appropriate time to have sex.

Every. Fucking. Weekend. It's like déjà vu 52 times a year.

You know, I often wonder how the relationship would be (or IF it would be) if he bloody spoke to me for a change. The other day, he told me he didn't even know I'd lived abroad...after TWO YEARS of dating me! Does he even know me?

Maybe next weekend we could play a few rounds of "two truths and a lie". Y'know, just to shake things up a little and see how well we really know each other! Maybe the winner can decide whether to carry on with this fucking JOKE we call a relationship!

And then he'll do something sweet. Out of the fucking blue. One of those big romantic gestures films tell us women love and feminists tell us are basically an excuse for men to be creepy. But it's always thoughtful and it always hits the mark. Bastard. Today he's filled the kitchen with peonies. I once told him the smell of peonies is my happy place. Did he really remember that? Or was it luck? I'm not sure, but all is forgiven...for now.

THE CHEATER by Rosemary Alogba

Cassie is aged 26, confident, sassy and proud. She is sitting at the bar waiting for her fiancé, as they are wanting to celebrate her qualification to practise law. She's talking to another customer who is also alone at the bar.

CASSIE: This is living! Tonight is all about me. This girl just passed the bar! That's right, I'm more than just beauty, I be brains too. But boy these last few years have not been easy, I'm talking late nights, early mornings, still working full time just to meet the odds, travelling back and forth, the judgements, the doubts, not to talk of a cheating fiancé… It's whatever, we're good now and I'm sure he's just stuck in some traffic, that's why he ain't here yet. Wait. There he is. Right. And there she is.

Oh Boy. Oh no. You see that piece getting out of his car? I'm not dreaming that, am I? This fiancé of mine is still cheating on me! Now he's coming over and he's going to give me some story about how she needed a lift. His co-worker. She's co-working her magic alright tonight.

You know what. Hell. No. Enough. I don't even need him no more, I don't need him. What am I doing here? The girls already told me, but I ignore them, I constantly forgive a cheater. I used to love everything about this guy, the efforts, the kindness, the understanding. Hell, this just made me turn a blind eye to every goddamn thing. But no one who loves you will put you through what this man has put me through, period! I can't keep thinking and waiting that he'll change. It's over. I'm going to tell him. Finally.

UNWILLINGLY ENGAGED by Denise Morton

Tabitha has just run away from her fiancé as fast as she could. She stands panting for breath, as she reflects on her next move.

TABITHA: There was a song in my heart as I viewed the Rhodes coastline at sunrise during a microlight flight experience. It was heavenly until I spotted them; the words "MARRY ME" written on the beach below, my boyfriend standing beside them. This had suddenly become one of the most traumatic days of my life.

I was not looking or feeling my best. Neither did I want to marry him. Not one bit. Now, a stronger person would have said "no", but I'm fearful of his violent streak. I spent the day being overwhelmed by the sick feeling of panic rising in my stomach, looking at my engagement ring which, it transpired later, I'd paid for.

The trouble is the more time I spent with him, the less I liked him. He's volatile, unpredictable and I'm starting to feel a bit frightened of him. I know he's into drugs and he's made some enemies. I was worried that if I stayed with him, I'd end up in trouble with the police at the door, or worse…and if he found out how I actually feel, he'd be furious. I didn't know how, but I needed to get out of that situation…and fast.

Then it occurred to me to run. I could just run. Literally run. I'm really fast. I used to win medals. So that's what I did. I ran. It's not the most sensible plan in the world, but it happened. I've not been home yet. And I don't plan to go back for a while, but right now, in this moment before I sort out the mess that is my life, I'm deliriously happy!

FREEDOM by Natasha Lewis.

Beatrice sips her gin and tonic.

BEATRICE. I loved university. Best days of my life. Little old me studying at a proper university. Drinking snakebite in the Students' Union every night. Freedom. Guys. It was bliss.

Pause.

I signed up for the Drama Society. I'd never really thought about doing any acting before and I'd never hung around with actor types. They were all so confident, I couldn't believe it. I surprised myself though. I was actually okay at it. At least that's what my friends said. I even got a part in the Christmas play. *An Ideal Husband.* Not a lead role or anything, but I had a few good scenes.

Pause.

That's when I met him. Richard Parkes. He was gorgeous. We were inseparable. We stopped studying, we stopped going out, we pretty much stopped doing anything really, we just lost ourselves in each other. They used to call us the "Campus LoveBugs". That's until I got pregnant.

Pause.

Well, I couldn't keep it could I? He said, “it would ruin my future”.

TRUTH AND LIES by Fiona Robertson

Debs is talking to her partner, Paul.

DEBS: I told some lies last night.

I was at the Asda tram stop, and this drunk guy swayed up to me, way too close for comfort, all whisky-breath and slurring. He reminded me of you in the bad days. He asked me for a cigarette. I said no, I don't smoke. Then he asked, "what's your name, are you married, where are you going?" I don't know where it all came from, but I said my name is Alison, I've been married to Steve for 15 years, and I'm going to Toton. All complete bollocks, obviously, but you know what, it felt great. I didn't have to be me for a moment. I could pretend none of it had happened.

I know you think I'm a saint for putting up with you, and yeah, you were the one telling the big lies, the proper lies about Jamie and the money and all that, but I lied too. Most of the time you were too drunk to notice. And I hated you for not noticing. How could you not notice how it was for me, how unsafe I felt? I hated you for not noticing how much I hated you.

You know what? I lied to you every day. When I said "I love you" what I really meant was, "I'm scared to death of being on my own so please don't leave me". When I said, "yeah, that was really good" what I actually meant was, "I only let you fuck me because you're so pissed you'll pass out afterwards and I'll get to watch what I want without you ranting on". I lied to you because I was embarrassed by you, afraid of you, angry with you. Fucking coward that I am.

Monologues About Family

MESSY PARENTAL LOVE by Tim Booth

On a bench in a city centre, Anna is talking to her 16-year-old niece, Mia.

ANNA: No, wait! Don't storm off, just hear me out. Please? It's just…there are things I want you to know, things about me, Mia. I know you've been through a lot, and I am so sorry, I can't imagine what it's been like. I mean shit, when I was 16 all I was worrying about was exams and sex. Yeah, sorry, that was…hmmm. Too much. I'm a mess, Mia. I know it probably looks like I've got my shit together but me and your mum, we aren't that different. Maybe it's genetics, I don't know.

Funny thing is your grandad always said it'd be me that went off the rails, not your mum. Not that funny, really. Well, he was half right. You see, the thing is… I'm an alcoholic, Mia. Yeah. Recovering. Trying. I've been sober for nearly four months now. It's been horrible. I'm miserable, and lonely. And I'm scared, really scared. I used to have fun, I think. But what if this boring, irritating, antisocial husk is all that's left? What if this is all there will ever be?

But hey, you know what? Still going, soldiering on, you know, one day, one step, and all that bollocks. Still whining. But then…then your mum tries to kill herself again and suddenly it's like I've got another teenager to look after. I mean, fuck! I'm like "how can I care for her when I don't even know how to look after me?" Listen, you want me to promise that I'll be here for you, but I don't know what the hell I'm doing and I probably never will. But I'm not going to stop trying to be here for you. Always. That's a promise.

TOAST by Brian Welby

Stan raises a toast to his favourite nephew.

STAN: Right then you bunch of pussies. Are we taking this seriously or what?

Pause.

What's that? I couldn't hear you over all that poncey whining just then. If you don't drink those shots, I'm going to ruin the lot of you. Every last fucking one of you. You bunch of absolute fucking wasters. That's it you little git! Get it down you! Right. Shut up Terrence. It's not your night, is it, you little gobshite. Wahay! Time for some fucking Champers boys!

Pause.

I would like to raise a toast to this tiny little tosspot next to me. He's never been good at much, bless him. Can't drink. Can't flog cars. He could kick a ball. Couldn't box though. And poor lad has got a tiny little penis. But he's alright. He's a good lad really, aren't you mate? And you've been like a son to me. Haven't you? You little shit stain. We've had some good times, haven't we mate?

Pause.

Well Tommy, you've finally done something useful with that minute todger of yours and the sad thing is, it's now the end of life as you know it. But it will be worth every second, I'm sure. So, make the most of it tonight young man. Because you won't be doing this for a while!

Pause.

Gentleman. Raise your glasses…to Tom's tiny cock!

SERIOUS SWIMMER by Adei Bundy

Michelle recounts an embarrassing moment.

MICHELLE. So I'm like 10 or 12. And I'm swimming and I'm doing amazing. I can feel that I'm ahead and I can hear my dad shouting (*In Dad's voice.*) "'Shell 'Shell give 'em hell!" (*In own voice.*) I knew I was going to win! Well, I have a secret weapon. Not drugs or anything like that. It's like a technique. Basically, I don't pee. Seriously, the whole day before a race, I didn't pee. It made me go well fast because I was running to the loo straight after!

So I'm going. I hit the wall and I'm on my last legs. Suddenly, it seems a really long way! A bit slips out. I feel it. I tense to try and stop it. I'm slowing down. (*In Dad's voice.*) "'Shell, 'Shell give 'em hell." (*In own voice.*) I tense and kick but it's all coming out and the water is going dark blue. The trail of dark blue liquid is following me to the finish. But then, my bladder lightens, and I get faster and faster. Give 'em hell! And I win!

I am mortified.

Pause.

But I win.

My dad scoops me up in my towel and I get my medal. Everyone looks at me in horror, but Dad just beams with pride. He didn't care, cos 'Shell gave them hell and although it's not the victory he imagined, he got what he wanted.

Pause.

And what's wrong with that?

THE DAY DAD LEFT By Lauren Williams

Anna is angry that her parents split up and firmly believes that's what led to her brother's death.

ANNA: You're joking? No! You're actually being serious! I don't believe this. Keeping secrets from your child is one thing, but confronting me with the truth like this is something else.

Today is significant. September 5th. The day I lost track of time. Smoking, drinking, partying. That's what happened to me. It's the day everything changed. My brother, Daniel. Your son. Gone! Killed in a car accident. And that was the final straw, the tragic results of your divorce.

It still hurts. I still cry. Scream even. Not being able to understand how I feel is messing up my head. My behaviour is self-destructive, but an off switch isn't an option for me. I'm scared I'm going to end up the same as Daniel. Tell me what to do. Please. Help me. September 5th was the day Dad left and everything stopped making sense.

A GOOD MAN by Daniel Staniland

Tom stands on a used car dealership forecourt.

TOM: Amy and I talked about having kids. You know, "trying". Well, I don't know why but...but I didn't think it would actually happen, well not for a while at least. I suppose I should have known better, shouldn't I?

Pause.

I mean, I'm working on a car lot, earning next to nowt and for what? To be a good man? Well, being a good man don't pay the bills, does it? How am I supposed to support a family? I still feel like a kid myself.

Pause.

I used to stay with my uncle Stan in the six weeks holidays. I was well excited to go and see him. It was a different world. Like a dream. His house, his car. I mean, he had a pool! And not just some cheap shitty plastic thing with leaves and crap floating around in it. Like a proper pool! Had my first drink there. My first fag. My first line of coke. I lost my virginity there. And she was stunning. I knew he paid for her, but it didn't matter. My dad had fucked off and that was my uncle's way of showing me he loved me.

Pause.

Stan was always there for me.

ROUTINES by Stella Lock

A wife stands in her kitchen.

WIFE: My husband will be back any minute. He has his dinner served at 6 o'clock on the dot. Soon as he walks through that door.

Everyone has routines, don't they? But my life is so predictable. So ordered. Literally not a stone left unturned.

My only escape has been browsing through holiday brochures. I imagine sandy beaches, posh hotels and exploring the world in luxurious comfort. Sometimes, I leave a holiday brochure on his desk, just a subtle hint. But he hates holidays. He just puts them in the bin. "What they got there, that we ain't got here?", he says. Any wonder I crave chaos and disorder?

Well, today is going to be extremely disordered. Because I've been keeping a little secret. You see, I've won the lottery. I have. Honestly! I know you probably don't believe me. I still don't quite believe it myself.

For the past 15 years, I have managed to hide my tickets in the bottom of my knitting basket. He doesn't knit, you see. Nor does he approve of "gambling". Ha!

I've already paid for my flight. Barbados. First class. Single. One way and I leave tomorrow!

I wonder how he'll take the news? Wine's poured. Ready to toast my new disordered, chaotic and unpredictable life.

Oh, that's his car. He's just pulled onto the drive. Wish me luck. Cheers!

BLACK FRIDAY by Tim Bryn Smith

Two men are in a shopping aisle. One is brandishing a roast chicken. John holds an oversized scented candle.

JOHN: Whoa! What do you think you are doing? Errr... Could you put that rotisserie chicken down please? Look, I did an Open University course in contract law, so I think I know when someone is trying to intimidate me with a hot food item. Right? We clearly both want this smelly candle. It's the last one and yeah, it's at a ridiculously low Black Friday price BUT if I don't return home with a Pineapple Fluff Bread Scented Yankee Candle within the hour, then my wife is going to go utterly ballistic and she's in her, like, 4th semester or something. She can't get enough of these things. It's mental. She's addicted. And this Banana Nut Loaf and Unicorn flavour is like the only one that will quench her insatiable thirst for scented wax. Her cravings bro! She's basically eating the wax straight of the out the jar like f-ing Haagen Dazs. It's messed up. I know! She's f-ing ravenous!

You see. I... I'm a... I really... She wants to leave me. I don't blame her, to be honest. I'm driving a '14 plate Renault Megane. She wants a Land Rover 'Envoke'. She deserves a Land Rover 'Envoke'. I can't afford those monthly instalments. I mean. She's amazing. I'm screwed. I don't think the baby's mine. There's a bloke at her gym. Alexis, I think his name is. He's got a sleeve of tattoos.

Sorry about that. I'm going on a bit now, aren't I? I tell you what. How about I put the Banana Biscuit and Toast flavour Wankee Candle down and you put that garlic and herb rotisserie chicken back down? No one gets assaulted. We can both walk away from this with our heads held high. Pride intact. Yeah? Okay? How's that for a Black Friday Deal?

He lowers candle back on to shelf.

Cool? Right... Easy does it, big guy.

He snaps the candle back up and runs off screaming.

Sorry mate! She'll f-ing kill me... Help! Please! Someone? Security?

THE SHADOW OF YOU by Wendy Gerrard–Tarpey

Claire is staring out of her window in the kitchen and thinking about what had happened the previous day.

CLAIRE: I saw you yesterday. I was in the coffee shop on the high street when you walked by with your wife, arm in arm. There you were, not a care in the world, laughing along with the woman who broke Mum's heart. You would never have guessed the torment and destruction that you caused in the life you once shared with us.

Even now, all these years later, you disgust me as a human being. I saw you hit Mum and so did Helen. We never forgot that. When Mum said you had to pay child support you refused, so the court said you had to see us every Saturday until we were 16. As soon as Helen reached that age you disappeared like you had just completed a contract. We never heard from you again, but I was glad to wash my hands of you because you failed us, you failed on so many levels.

Helen and I are strong, loving, determined, courageous and successful women. You would be so, so proud of us, but you don't know us and we don't care because we don't need you, or the validation we once craved from you, anymore.

Revelations

RED FLAG by Helena Harrison

Leanne is talking to her careers advisor.

LEANNE: I think the first red flag was the interview. I say "interview". I was greeted by a man who didn't actually introduce himself, he just said "follow me" and asked me to fill out a form. The form asked for my personal details, contact information, employment history, education – you know, all the stuff that you'd easily find on my CV which I had emailed and also printed out and brought along with me. I was then asked two questions:

"Right, so when can you start?"

"Oh, erm, ASAP to be honest. Immediately, yeah. I can start immediately."

"Great. And do you own safety boots?"

"Do I look like I own safety boots? No, I don't. But I can get some!"

"Brill. Do you have any questions?" I mean at this point I probably should have asked some basics. What is the job? What will I actually be doing? But of course, I just said:

"No, that's great thank you!"

"Brill. If you just complete the English test on the back then ya can go."

English test? The job advert hadn't said anything about a test. Shit. It's not that I'm bad at English, I mean I am English and I can speak it to an adequate level but I just really hate tests. I either overthink the question or don't read it properly in the first place and get myself in a right tizz. Anyway. I turn the piece of paper over to see a drawing of a circle.

Question one: what shape is this? Ah. Think I'm going to be okay. Oh and it's multiple choice, excellent. Circle. Question two: what colour is the shape? Well, it's printed in black and white so? Oh god.

"Excuse me, sorry, for question two it asks for the colour but…"

"Just put red, duck."

"Right, okay, thank you. Red."

As I say, first red flag. A literal one. The second red flag was more metaphorical.

"When you've finished with the test, love, you can get undressed in this room. The door to the right. Then Danny will be along with the camera." It was at this point I realised I probably didn't want the job, whatever it was…

BEST FRIENDS by Spencer Hague

Stephen is a moderately successful person, with a beautiful wife and two daughters whom he loves more than life itself. He is seeing his therapist for the first time.

STEPHEN: I wish I could reset time to before the moment I found my best friend dead in his bedroom. If I could just go back then maybe this pain would stop. When someone close to you dies, you don't instantly feel how you think you'd feel. When I saw him, it wasn't overwhelming sadness, but pure, extreme shock, mixed with confusion and hope. Hope that he was just asleep, playing some sick joke. Until I felt how stone cold he was...

I'd always just assumed that it was time that makes you a best friend. But could being a best friend actually be based on your actions? Because my actions as a friend, now that I look back, were not those of a best friend. I wouldn't always stick up for him against the bullies, didn't always have his back in arguments and sometimes would use him as my own personal punching bag... Actually, now I think about it, maybe he was a better friend than I.

He WOULD stick up for me, he DID have my back, he never retaliated aggressively no matter how hard I would hit him. He always stood by my side, regardless of how much of a bad friend I was! So, it's not until now, ten years after his death, that I realise maybe he was MY best friend, but I wasn't his. Have I been grieving all this time as a false best friend? If I had the chance to go back in time, I could be that friend he always deserved. If only I'd realised that earlier, he might still be alive.

ACTOR'S LIFE by Rhys Beardsley

Mark ponders the reality of making it as an actor.

MARK: My careers advisor laughed when I told him I wanted to be an actor. "Have you considered any real jobs?", he said. REAL JOBS? I wish I'd told him to f-off. It would have been worth getting expelled for. Just to see the look on his smug fat face.

Career wise? It's not been too bad. But no, not great recently. Well, nothing for over two years. Apart from a week's T.I.E job warning kids about the dangers of sniffin' Tippex. I do ask myself sometimes why I carry on. Why things didn't turn out the way I thought they would. Obviously, I thought it would have been better...a few more theatre bits, a little more success, a few lines on Corrie even.

I did think about re-training or working with my brother. Landscape gardening. But I just couldn't bring myself to do it. Friends come up to you and say, "Have you been on telly yet"? Randoms say, "Have I seen you in anything?" Well, you would know if you'd seen me, because you'd have seen me in it, wouldn't you? You knob.

I was in *Crossroads,* in the background. You could see a bit of my arm. My brother says I should "stop loafing about". Well, I've got a walk-on in *Doctors* next month. I might even get a line. I know the director, well, I mean I follow her on Twitter. She's never liked any of my posts, but when she sees me on set she's bound to recognise me. I re-post my headshots every week, so there's no way she's not seen them. Bound to offer me at least one line, isn't she? I hope she still recognises me in a surgical mask.

PRAYERS ANSWERED by Foteini Eleni Karampali

Genevieve is praying at the foot of the bed.

GENEVIEVE: I know I said I could make life easier for myself. I know I said I would try to look on the positive side, that I would stop overthinking things and being self-destructive. But there I was again in my own prison. I couldn't pretend anymore. I wasn't happy. I wasn't even close to it. I was sick of crying every night before I sleep and every morning when I woke up.

Only you knew what was going on in my mind. The chaos had to stop. I told myself I'd pray for one last time to stop these nightmares, to pause these dark and brooding thoughts. TO SHUT THESE VOICES UP. And it worked! It shouldn't have been a surprise; this test of my faith, that we both responded to it. Did you, my God, make it stop? I hardly dare to imagine that I have experienced the sublime; a golden silence that was mine alone. I have been blessed with a second chance.

DISNEYLAND by Claudia Langley-Mills

Michelle reminisces about school life.

MICHELLE: I remember at school, my teacher asked us what we wanted to be when we were older. We were all about five or six at the time. Most kids said they wanted to be doctors or pop stars. One boy said he wanted to be a superhero. I couldn't really think of anything, so I just said I wanted to be a princess. Everyone laughed at me and said you can't be a princess. My teacher asked if I wanted to be anything else and I said no, so she moved on.

Afterwards, I thought about what I'd said. What could be better than falling in love with a prince and living happily ever after?

I thought anybody could be a princess, even me. Not necessarily in a literal sense obviously.

But maybe they were right. And I'm just a fool.

LEAVING DERBY by Morgan Delahayes

Wednesday morning in the office. A Frenchman talks to an Englishman.

PASCAL: *(In French.)* Putain, j'm'en bats les couilles, j'me barre de c'te ville de merde! Oh…you've not been practising your French have you Frank? I was saying I'm moving to Nottingham. Because, I tell you, I can't stay another night in Derby! Do you know what happened to me yesterday? Classic Tuesday night. I went out with the guys to get a couple of pints, and around 10 o'clock, I decided to go home. I'm walking in this not at all creepy empty street - with a strong piss smell - when I see a guy. A skinny meth-head-looking kind of guy, leaning on a wall. I see him. He sees me. But it's too late to change direction now, so I walk slowly, avoiding eye contact. Hoping I won't get stabbed repeatedly in the face. You know, like we all do.

As I get closer to him, I can see that he's rolling what appears to be a huge joint. And I really don't know why, but I find it quite reassuring. So, my mistake, I started smiling. And he smiles back. It was then I realised that he was missing a LOT of teeth. Next thing, he engages in conversation. *(In strange voice.)* "Do you have a lighter?"

Who am I to refuse help to someone in need? So, I hand him my lighter and he goes like *(In strange voice)* "Oh thanks, you're so sweet! What are you doing now?" I reply "I'm just going home. It's getting late and I have to go to work in the morning."

He says, "Am I hearing an accent? Where are you from mate?"

"I'm French", I say.

"French? Ooooh sacrebleu! What can I do for you, my dear monsieur?" So I say, "Nothing really, I'm just gonna go home". But then he says, "Are you sure? Come on, I'll buy you a drink".

I'm like, "Thanks, but I really need to go home now". And then he says, "Do you want me to suck your dick?".

Oh la la putain de merde! Can you believe this!? I mean how rude is it to offer a blow job to someone you've just met in the street. On a Tuesday night? People have to work in the morning. They'll get tired. And that's not fair! That's not fair!

Then again. The guy had no teeth. Right?

INTERVIEW by Samantha Badman

Sally sits across from the panel.

SALLY. Well, that's a very good question. I suppose something inside of me broke. My "soul". If you believe in that sort of thing, which I don't. Not really. But something definitely changed inside me. Where I'd been afraid to die before, I suddenly realised it didn't matter…my experiences won't live on after me, the world won't change. Life means nothing…in the grand scheme of things, there is no meaning. No purpose to existence. So why should I try? Why should I make the effort to pretend that everything is fine? Whatever "fine" is.

We all do it. Don't we? Every day, meaningless platitudes.

"How are you?"

"Oh, I'm fine, yourself?"

" Yeah, fine thanks." But what does that actually mean? "Fine"? It means, I'm able to hide my fears, insecurities, and prejudices from the world, so I can go unnoticed. Untargeted.

The next time a colleague asked me "Alright?" I said, "No actually. I'm not. I'm not alright. I am broken, I'm empty. I'm hollow and there's this void inside that I can't fill up. The world is going to shit, and I just don't see the point in being alive anymore". What an expression! You should have seen it! Shock, concern and surprise all rolled into one. There's no emoji for that!

I'd been hiding it and it felt good to let it out. To admit the truth. Telling him didn't change me. It didn't "fix" me...but it felt right not to hide it. It's not that I want to die, I just don't care if I do.

So. In answer to your question. That's why I think I am perfect for this job. Bomb disposal.

Crime and Legal

FIGHT OR FLIGHT by Jay Bradley

Dale sits on a bench outside the courtroom waiting for his solicitor.

DALE: Why did I do it? Boredom, 32 years and 10 months of utter drudgery. Wake up at 6; shower; get dressed; eat breakfast; drive to work; stand on the line; lunch at 12.30; cheese sandwich; plain crisps; fun sized chocolate bar; leave work at 4; home by 4.30; microwave meal for one; watch the soaps; make tomorrow's lunch; cheese sandwich; plain crisps; fun sized chocolate bar; masturbate; shower then bed. 32 years and 10 months… sprinkled with the odd distraction, but nothing noteworthy, that's why it had to be something extreme, the complete opposite, an outrageous thing, utterly removed from my boring, humdrum life.

I used to pass her in the morning as she stood waiting for the bus. Even though she worked on line 3, and I was on line 1, I didn't know her. I never stopped to offer her a lift…not until yesterday.

It was raining. I didn't offer her a lift because it was raining, but because it gave me an excuse to. Nicky, her name was Nicky, very petite. I'm guessing, subconsciously, that's another reason why I picked her, although to be fair she was surprisingly strong, especially towards the end. Fight or flight response, that's what they call it when the adrenalin kicks in. The other bits, that was pure theatre, something for the masses, at least now we'll both be remembered. Maybe she would have appreciated that. Or maybe not.

32 years and 10 months. That's what you get for murder.

HEY, LOOKIN GOOD FOR AN OLD UN by Linda Wilmott

Judith is sitting opposite a WPC in an interview room at Brighton John Street Police Station.

JUDITH: His profile said he was 65, but I thought he looked a lot older than his photos. As he crossed the road towards me, I noticed what great hair he had and he was tall too. Thank God I could keep my heels on, makes a change. As he got closer, I admired his jacket, designer I think, and I also caught a distinct whiff of mothballs. But he was still cute, you know, for an old un! He was an artist, you know. I ALWAYS fall for creative types. All talk and no money.

It bothered me that he didn't seem too interested in ME. I was waiting for some clue...but nothing. Not a wink, a hug, a kiss. A big fat NOTHING. Instead, he always talked about stuff he needed. It was like his shopping list. Could I pick up this for him, could I take him to the chemist, the supermarket? He didn't have a car, you see.

I felt sorry for him, separated from his kids. Unable to reach them in Scotland unless I drove him. We met up eight times and on our last day out we went to a lovely country house and had lunch. I paid...again. But then, I was enjoying myself so much, despite how he was with me. But driving home, well, I just had this "moment". I felt vulnerable. I can do this I thought, he IS worth it.

As I reached close to touch, I hesitated, fingers a little shaky, and a rush of adrenaline came over me. I HIT SEND. £5,000 resting on Cupid's arrows winged its way towards his account (*Resigned sigh.)* Well, he needed the car to go and see his kids, didn't he? And he needed me.

FORCED by Kyle Chaplin.

Danny is at the police station, reporting a sex crime.

DANNY: He did it, you know. Whatever story he gave you, it's all lies. We were at a party and everyone was pretty drunk. Shots and all that. My friend Lily was passed out in the corner. She's usually the first one to fall because she can't handle her alcohol like she used to. I was walking to the bathroom and someone followed me in and locked the door behind us. It was him.

I asked him what he was doing, and he said, "Whatever I want". He pushed me against the wall and pressed himself against me. The hairs of his beard scraping my skin as he forced himself on me. He pulled my trousers down and cornered me in the cubicle. It all gets a bit blurry after that. I think I must've blacked out.

When I came round, I was on the floor, my trousers wrapped around my ankles. I could see blood. When I looked up, he was just stood there. He knelt down beside me and said if I told anyone, he'd hurt me...really bad. He told me that if I told the police, he'd hurt my family. I was terrified. I didn't know what else to do. So, I cleaned myself up as best I could and I ran.

I've replayed that night over and over again in my head. Did I do something to lead him on? Or was I just easy prey? Whatever the reason, I can't do it anymore. I had to tell someone. Please, for me, and any other person he may or may not have done this to. Bring. Him. Down.

HIT THEM HARD By Adam Brailsford

Jason is addressing a judge in the Crown Court.

JASON: Violence is sometimes the answer Your Honour and I'm an expert on violence, me. I've been at it my whole life. There's some people that I should've fucking hit when I didn't. And there's some people who I didn't fucking hit hard enough.

When I were seven my Dad used to take me boxing. So, I were getting smacked in the face on a Tuesday, a Thursday and on a Sunday. Bosh Bosh Bosh.

Those pricks cutting down the rainforest for profit. They're the ones who deserve violence. Don't they know it's the lungs of the Earth. I'm going to get the cunt who's in charge of that and strangle the bastard so that he can't breathe and tell him this is what it will fucking be like if he carries on cutting down the trees. It'll work better than any tree hugger tying themselves to a tree.

My dad is a problem, but he gave me a solution and my expertise in the use of violence to rehabilitate gets that problem solved. So, do you get it now? You know what I done was for the greater good, the first step towards fixing the planet. So, you gonna give me parole or what?

MORE LEGAL SEX PLEASE by Tom Russell

Alex is a middle-aged barrister, practising in criminal law. He was unwell a few years ago after a breakdown and had some time off work. He feels that his career has not advanced as it might have done. He is a little cynical as he shares recent experiences over a drink with an old friend, also in the legal profession.

ALEX: I've wanted more sex for a few years now. But the clerks have been reluctant. I'm not sure whether it was worry for my health or embarrassment for the greater good of chambers. Probably the latter.

Anyway. Surprise, surprise. Completely out of the blue last month, I was given a rape. It was an eleventh-hour return from Herbert, but I was still delighted. Years with no sex. Then bang. A lovely rape. Bog standard. No aggravating features. No DNA. Just a straightforward he said/she said. I celebrated hard with Polly and Andy at Gastro's.

The client was so funny when I saw him in the cells. He said, and I'm quoting: "It couldn't have been me. Have you seen the state of her? I don't do fat birds and I don't like tats. So I wouldn't be seen dead with her."

Anyway, we got cracking in front of Mackenzie. And he was doing his usual thing. Looking down his nose at everyone. Gave the prosecution a hard time. "Is this really capable of proof Mr Sedgwick?"

Turned out it was. I cross-examined for hours. Hours. But all the time my mind was drifting back to what happed in 2015. I couldn't focus. I remembered the humiliation of standing frozen outside Court 7 at the Bailey. Unable to speak. Staring at my shoes. I saw myself sitting alone on the stone steps of Blackfriars Bridge with my head in my hands.

I know what they thought, the solicitors, the judge, Sedgwick and his junior. The client, the poor client. His face. There was no case and I created one. Seven years. Seven fucking years in Pentonville. Because he got me. Because he got me and he should have got Herbert.

I'm a fraudster next week. Which seems appropriate.

NO OFFENCE by Tim Bryn Smith

Wahnnetta is a brash Glaswegian, getting irate at a traffic warden.

WAHNNETTA: Oh sorry. I'll get out of your way mate, so you can keep ruining my life! Just walk round me mate. You've got legs ain't ya? Walk round me!

Wahnnetta side steps and flaps her arms around.

You can't "get round me"? You saying I'm chubby? You're so chubby, you could sell shade mate. You're so fat, you're leaving footprints IN the pavement. I can lose weight if I wanted to mate but you'll ALWAYS be ugly… In fact, if I had a face like yours, I'd sue my parents. The last time I saw summat that looked like you, I flushed it. If ugly were a crime, you'd get a life sentence mate.

No reaction from the traffic warden. She realises she's not going to win. The warden taps on his device.

Okay. I'm sorry. Please don't do that. It's my boy's birthday tomorrow. I was on my way to get him a present. Please mate. Come on. Please.

The traffic warden shrugs "I'm just doing my job".

"You're just doing your job." You're a parasite. You're scum! Proper scumbag mate… Go on, keep talking, someday you'll say something intelligent! If you really spoke your mind, you'd be speechless mate. Write yer bloody ticket. You robot. You clone. I don't care. Fine me. Go on. Fine me… Please don't fine me.

The traffic warden continues to write the ticket, huffs and rolls his eyes.

Whatever mate, roll your eyes. Keep rolling them, perhaps you'll find a brain back there. I'd give you a slap, but it'd be animal abuse.

The traffic warden looks threatened.

You think that's a "threat"? That's not a threat! Just LOLs mate! Don't call the police. Come on I was only joking. Bants mate. Just bants! Look. I'm parked on single yellows and it's well gone 6pm. You can't give me a ticket for that can you?

The traffic warden nods.

You can?! You must have been born on a motorway mate because that's where accidents happen. You're the reason the gene pool needs a lifeguard. Your birth certificate is an apology letter from the condom factory!

Wahnnetta has a look of deep shock and embarrassment.

Erm…actually mate…are you writing that ticket for the blue Citroen? Oh… Ah… No… Mine's the red Ford just there. Sorry mate. Not my car. No offence. Thanks anyway. Bye!

ABOUT THE CURATORS

Tim Bryn Smith

After graduating from the BAFTA winning Television Workshop, Tim pursued a career as an actor, winning roles in a number of shows including *Hollyoaks, Holby City, Heartbeat, The Bill, Teachers, Dream Team, Mr Eleven, Charity Shop Sue* and *Doctors*, plus various roles on stage and radio. He moved into film and TV production as a director/producer with Fourmost Films and later with Spool Films. Tim was recruited to help launch the ambitious new digital channel Notts TV which enjoyed great success during his tenure, attracting a regular audience of over 1.5 million viewers. As well as developing and producing a number of new concept TV shows, his commercial production credits include work for Virgin, Redbull, BBC iPlayer, Barclays, Vauxhall and Chevrolet as well as a slate of commissions for local businesses and charity organisations.

Tim is passionate about sharing the life-enhancing benefits of actor training, so in 2010 he founded The Actors Workshop Nottingham and later The Actors Workshop Online, so that the learning experience could be enjoyed anywhere in the world. These accessible teaching facilities have not only trained thousands of adults in the skills required for careers in stage and screen - many of the workshop's alumni can now be seen plying their trade across the entertainment industry - but has also improved the creativity, confidence and self-esteem of all those who actively participate.

Looking to offer students the chance to create professional showreel material, Tim's screen experience led him to pioneer Screen School, an intensive screen acting course which culminates in the production of a series of extremely high-quality portfolio scenes. Tim's eye for detail, appetite for finding emotional truth and his extensive professional experience both in front of and behind the camera has been an asset to countless students for over two decades.

Tim first met writer Sara Bodinar whilst producing and directing *Sketch Up*, an original format show for Notts TV. The pair have worked numerous times together since, including co-producing a theatrical production of *Marriage & Murder* and the feature film *TAWN-19*, as well as developing hundreds of monologues and duologues for actors' showreels over the years. Tim is excited and proud to collaborate with Sara and the authors of *Monologues For Showreels*.

Sara Bodinar

Sara got her first literary agent while studying for an MA in Spanish literature at the University of Nottingham and was a published author by the time she graduated. However, it wasn't until she was writing a weekly column for the Nottingham Evening Post that her theatre and film career suddenly took off. Her political satire *There Be Migrants Here* (produced by Minty Fresh Productions), about two Brits seeking asylum in Romania, enjoyed a couple of packed-out nights at London's

503 Theatre. Then, her short film *Rambling On* (produced by Sonder Pictures) picked up a number of awards and screenings on the festival circuit.

Since then, Sara has worked on many different feature films and TV programmes as a screenwriter and script editor at film studios and production companies around the world. She is now represented by Red Talent Management. TV career highlights include writing for *Lego Discover, Secrets of a Slay Queen, Spectrum London, Zayn and Zayna's Little Farm,* and upcoming travel show, *Where is She?* She is also proud to be an active part of the in-house writing teams at film studios in London and Zambia, working on both box office hits and independent releases.

Theatre is also an important part of Sara's work. She is a member of the Nottingham Playhouse Theatre's participation team. She led the Young Critics workshop during her first year in the team, and now leads an Encore play readers workshop. A play she co-wrote with Dan McGarry, called *Seeking Isolde,* enjoyed a UK tour, and she adored writing the scripts for the Young Urban Actors 2019 Theatre Festival. Her latest theatre venture is *FIB,* a brand new Arts Council funded musical set in Liverpool, which will have its first performance in the summer of 2021.

Sara has been working with actors for many years to help them develop unique showreel scripts. Initially through Shout Showreels, and then with Tim at The Actors Workshop Online, she enjoys the challenge of creating a script that shows off an individual actor to their best advantage.

Devising theatre and developing scenes with actors, along with her dramatic writing experience and production work, has given Sara an insight into the types of monologues that will greatly enhance any showreel and catch a casting director's eye. She is thrilled to collaborate with Tim Bryn Smith on this book. The pair have worked on many exciting projects together, with much more planned for the future. Their aim, in curating this volume of monologues, is to provide actors with high quality scripts that will take them, via their showreels, to the next level in their career.

About the Actors Workshop Online

The Actors Workshop provides an opportunity for adults aged 18 and over to explore and develop the necessary skills for careers in film, television and radio. Through acting workshops, drama classes and private one-to-one tuition we strive to both nurture new talent and enhance the skills of experienced actors.

Since 2010 many members of The Actors Workshop have benefitted from casting opportunities in film, television, voice over, corporate videos and more. Our sessions are delivered by professional facilitators, teachers and lecturers aiming to bring both quality and variety. Recent sessions have included film acting, physical theatre, audition technique, Meisner Technique, Perdekamp Emotional Method, Practical Aesthetics, Sword Fighting, Musical Theatre, Chekhov and more. Weekly workshops run in the evenings for both inexperienced and professional actors.

If you would like to be part of The Actors Workshop visit: actorsworkshoponline.com.

Printed in Great Britain
by Amazon

62644187R00093